Business Economics:
Microeconomics
for **A2**

2nd Edition

Robert Nutter

ınforme

Contents

Firms

Firms are defined as business organisations where decisions are made. They are of particular interest to economists because, as business organisations, they are typically engaged in the production of goods and services. In other words, firms combine scarce resources (factors of production) in order to produce a valuable output which satisfies human needs or wants. Factors of production are classified under the headings of land (covering all natural resources), labour (human resources), capital (man made goods for use in producing further output) and enterprise (the entrepreneur who organises the other three resources). These resources are finite in quantity and hence scarce relative to infinite human needs and wants.

Profit

This is the excess of a firm's revenue over its costs. From an economic point of view, cost means the opportunity cost of the factors of production used (i.e. the value of each factor when employed in its next best use).

A money payment for a factor of production will generally be a fairly accurate reflection of its opportunity cost, because this is the minimum payment required to ensure the factor is not lost to another use (often called transfer earnings), and one would not expect a firm to pay more than necessary for a factor's services. Consider, for example, a machine available for hire. Suppose, for the sake of simplicity, that only two firms would like to hire the machine and that it will generate £400 revenue per week for firm A and £300 for firm B. If the rent rises above £300 per week, firm B will drop out of the bidding. We therefore expect firm A to hire the machine, at a rent of marginally above £300 per week. This £300 per week represents the opportunity cost of the machine, as it would generate this sum in its next best use (with firm B).

To find the full economic cost of production we must also include a sum to represent the opportunity cost of factors of production for which no money payment is made. These may be termed **imputed costs**. Consider, for example, the person who gives up a job paying £40,000 per annum in order to set up his/her own business. This £40,000 given up is a real cost of the new business, although no money changes hands to cover this cost.

Accordingly: Economic cost = money cost + imputed cost

The accountant's measure of profit takes into account only money costs such as wages, raw materials and power. Thus, his measure of profit exceeds that of the economist, i.e. when the economic profit is zero, the accounting profit is positive. This is described as a situation in which **normal profit** is made. If revenue were to fall further, it would not be sufficient to cover the opportunity costs of all factors of production. These factors would then, in the long run, move to their next best use. Normal profit, therefore, is the minimum accounting profit required to keep factors of production in their current use. Any profit over and above this level is termed abnormal profit, supernormal or economic profit. For the entrepreneur normal profit represents his/her transfer earnings and abnormal profit represents economic rent.

To summarise:

Accounting Profit = Sales Revenue − Accounting Cost (money cost)

Economic Cost = Accounting Cost (money cost) + Opportunity Cost of the factors of production (imputed cost)

Economic Profit (abnormal profit) = Sales Revenue − Economic Cost

Resources will be attracted to those activities where abnormal profits can be earned.

Question 1.1

A recruitment consultant resigns from his £50,000 per annum position in order to set up his own business. In the process of setting up the new business, he invests £60,000 of his own capital. During the first year, premises are rented for £30,000 while the only other costs are administration (£15,000) and the salaries of two junior consultants (each £25,000). Assume that in a typical year the owner of the new firm would have received £10,000 worth of bonuses in his old salaried job. The annual interest rate is 5%. The revenue of the new business in the first year is £150,000.

(a) On the basis of these figures, identify the accounting costs and economist's imputed costs of the business.

(b) Calculate and describe the profit made last year.

(c) Repeat part (b), using an interest rate of 3%.

(d) In general, what market conditions must hold for supernormal profit to be made?

(The final part of the question should only be attempted if you have studied the theory of the firm – see Section C.)

The entrepreneur

The entrepreneur is an economic agent who perceives market opportunities and assembles factors of production to exploit them in a firm. In the static, neo-classical economics of perfect competition there is no place for the entrepreneur since it is assumed that there is perfect information and freedom of entry. Following the work of Frank Knight it can be argued that the pure function of an entrepreneur is to deal with uncertainty in the dynamic, imperfect, real world in which profit is a return to uncertainty and entrepreneurship is inseparable from control of the firm in which he operates. The essence of the entrepreneur, therefore, is that he/she is alert to gaps in the market, which others do not see, and is able to raise the finance and resources required by a firm in order to exploit the market that he/she initiates. If successful he/she will make a **supernormal/abnormal** profit that will later reduce to a normal profit, as new competitors are attracted into the market. In this conception, the pure function of an entrepreneur is as a fourth factor of production. Economists have attributed other functions than risk-taking to the entrepreneur: invention; the provision of risk capital and management, for example. Though not part of the pure entrepreneurial function, which is remunerated by profit, all these functions may be embodied in the owner of a small business. His/her remuneration may be made up of rent as an owner of land, interest as a return on capital, a wage or salary for his/her management function, and therefore as a return for his/her labour, and profit as a return for his/her entrepreneurship.

Good recent examples of successful entrepreneurs include Charles Dunstone who founded Carphone Warehouse, Anita Roddick (Body Shop), Richard Branson (Virgin), Stelios Haji-Ioannou (easyJet), Martha Lane Fox (Last Minute.com), Michael O'Leary (Ryanair) and James Dyson the vacuum and washing machine inventor. Most entrepreneurs have found the going tough at times. Trevor Bayliss the inventor of the clockwork radio originally found it difficult to get financial backers for his idea, Freddie Laker's airline collapsed in the early 1980's as did Sophie Mirman's Sock Shop chain in the early 1990's. However, the most successful entrepreneurs of recent years must surely be Sergey Brin and Larry Page who founded the internet search engine 'Google'. In the ten years up to 2008 Google turned itself into the world's biggest media business acquiring YouTube in the process.

Other notable entrepreneurs in recent years are also internet related. In 1995 Pierre Omidyar and Phil Fischner founded e-Bay, and in 2004 Mark Zuckerberg founded the social networking site Facebook which was recently floated on the NASDAQ at $38 per share.

A recent entrepreneurial success has been Will King with his company King of Shaves. King was made

Fair trade in coffee is an example of social entrepreneurship.

redundant in the early 1990s and started work on a shaving oil product which eased the pain of shaving–something he suffered from. The company grew from strength to strength producing a range of men's toiletries. The King of Shaves brand in 2009 was stocked in approximately 30,000 stores worldwide including the United States, Japan, Australia, New Zealand, Brazil and South Africa. The company's turnover almost doubled between 2007 and 2008.

In the £400m-a-year UK wet razors and blades market, Gillette has an estimated 80% to 85% share. King's company, which sold its first bottle of shaving gel in 1993, now has 10% of the UK market for wet shaving products and has made a small start in what was thought to be an impregnable competitive arena for razors dominated by Gillette and Wilkinson Sword.

One of Britain's most famous entrepreneurs of recent years, James Dyson wants a new generation of entrepreneurs who are inventors. He has warned that Britain is lagging behind its competitors in the field of invention and technology. According to Dyson "the US files 19 times more patents than us, South Korea seven times more, China nine times more – we have stopped inventing things. Pharmaceutical companies are almost the only ones left."

The government introduced the StartUp loans programme in 2012 which is targetted at 18-24 year olds who find difficulties when applying for loans from banks. Typical loans will be about £2,500 with interest charged at inflation plus 3 per cent. The loan will have to be repaid in five years. It is hoped that the scheme will launch 30,000 start-ups.

The government has also lent its financial support to 'peer to peer' lending where small businesses link directly to individuals and organisations with the latter lending money to the former. This enables small high risk ventures to have access to loan finance that would not be provided by the banks.

Social entrepreneurship has been more prominent since the start of the twenty-first century. The social entrepreneur runs firms that tackle social or environmental issues while also attempting to make a profit.

A social enterprise is a business that trades for a social and/or environmental purpose. It will have a clear sense of its 'social mission': which means it will know what difference it is trying to make, who it aims to

help, and how it plans to do it. It will bring in most or all of its income through selling goods or services. And it will also have clear rules about what it does with its profits, reinvesting these to further the 'social mission'.

Social enterprises come in many shapes and sizes from large national and international businesses to small community based enterprises. But they all:

(i) Are businesses that aim to generate their income by selling goods and services, rather than through grants and donations; (ii) Are set up to specifically make a difference; (iii) Reinvest the profits they make in their social mission.

The Big Issue, the Eden Project and Jamie Oliver's restaurant Fifteen which helps socially excluded young people are examples of social enterprises. The Annual Survey of Small Businesses UK estimated in 2010 that there are approximately 68,000 social enterprises in the UK contributing at least £24bn to the economy. Social enterprises are estimated to employ about 800,000 people.

Britain is one of the most attractive countries in which to set up a new business. Researchers at the Legatum Institute, have recently looked at the best countries to become an entrepreneur and these are:

1. Denmark
2. Sweden
3. United States
4. Finland
5. United Kingdom
6. Norway
7. Ireland
8. Singapore
9. Iceland
10. Canada

According to Legatum, to be a good entrepreneurial base a country needs "a strong entrepreneurial climate in which citizens can pursue new ideas and opportunities for improving their lives, leading to higher levels of income and wellbeing." The Legatum researchers looked at entrepreneurial environments, innovative activities and access to opportunity.

Question 1.2

Read the passages on the previous pages before responding to the following:

(a) Explain the claim that the function of an entrepreneur is risk-taking.

(b) How is it that there is only a role for an entrepreneur if the market is imperfect?

(c) "Entrepreneurship is the fourth factor of production". What is meant by this statement?

(d) There has been much talk in recent years about the development of an 'enterprise culture'. Why might this be considered important?

(e) Research a well known entrepreneur. In what sense is he or she so?

Why is profit important in a free market economy?

From the preceding analysis it is clear that profit fulfils some important functions:

1. It rewards risk takers such as shareholders and entrepreneurs.

2. It provides a stimulus to innovation to introduce new products and new production techniques.

3. It provides a source of funds for investment and research and development (retained profit).

4. It sends signals to potential investors and entrepreneurs because resources are drawn towards the production of goods where profits can be earned. This helps to allocate resources efficiently.

Unit 2: **The birth and growth of firms**

Measures of the size of a firm

There are a number of ways in which we can attempt to measure the size of a firm. These include: (1) Sales turnover; (2) Numbers employed; (3) Market share; (4) Stock market value (market capitalisation); (5) The value of its assets.

It does not follow that all five measures above move in the same direction. It is important to remember that some firms may have a low value of fixed assets but a high turnover, e.g. lastminute.com, and some firms may have a relatively small number of workers but a high turnover, e.g. an oil company such as Shell.

Types of firm

In the private sector there are various types of firm as defined by their legal structure. The sole trader is a firm owned by one person who usually makes all the decisions, although there may be other people employed by the firm. The partnership is owned by between two and twenty partners who enter into a partnership agreement. Some partners play no active part in the running of the business and are called sleeping partners. Profits are shared between the partners usually in proportion to their investment. Sole traders are often small shops and partnerships and are typically found among dentists and small building firms. Both types of business have **unlimited liability** which means that the owners are liable in full for all the debts of the business, although there are some exception provisions for partners in the form of limited liability partnerships.

Shareholders in a limited company who elect a board of directors to run the business on a day-to-day basis own a limited company. The shareholders have limited liability which means that their liability for the firm's debts is limited to the amount they invested in the business. Unlike unlimited liability the shareholders cannot lose their personal possessions if the firm is placed into receivership. There are two types of limited company, **private limited** (with Ltd after their name) and **public limited** (with PLC after their name). In a private limited company shareholders cannot sell their shares without permission, thus unlike a PLC, shares are not traded openly. A PLC's shares are traded on the Stock Exchange and shareholders are free to sell their shares whenever they like in what is essentially a second hand market. The share price of quoted PLCs will rise or fall depending on the forces of demand and supply, which are operating on the Stock Market. However both types of limited companies are governed by the similar rules of a joint stock company laid down in the **Articles and Memorandum of Association**. The Board of Directors of a limited company is elected by the shareholders to whom they recommend a dividend (share of the profits).

Many private limited companies are small family businesses and in some the shareholders and board members are the same people. However, there are some large private companies such as Virgin, Mars and Arcadia (which owns British Home Stores). PLCs are usually large businesses such as Marks and Spencer and British Airways. Interestingly and significantly private companies now control greater parts of the UK economy and in 2005 the takeover by the Glazier family of Manchester United PLC involved the Glaziers using borrowed money to buy a controlling interest in the club. Once they owned 90% of the shareholding they forced the remaining shareholders to sell to them; they also de-listed United from the Stock Exchange with the company reverting to private ownership. The trend towards private company status even among larger companies is partly explained by the complex rules and regulations associated with the corporate governance of PLCs. Many well known household names are now delisted having been taken over by **private equity firms**. Alliance Boots was initially a British PLC *and* listed on the London Stock Exchange. In 2007 it was bought out in a private equity transaction. In 2008 the trading business was transferred to a Swiss limited company, which is a wholly owned subsidiary of a British company, AB Acquisitions Holdings

Limited, which is owned by the private equity firm Kohlberg Kravis Roberts (KKR). The Stock Exchange has often been criticised for fostering an image of short-termism in British industry. Institutional investors such as pension funds and insurance companies have allegedly pressured quoted companies to pay high dividends at the expense of retained profit.

Franchises have become increasingly popular in recent years. The franchiser has a business plan which the franchisee must follow. The franchiser who receives royalty payments from the franchisee's income often provides the premises, training, advertising and materials. There are also many non-profit making organisations such as **mutual organisations** which are found in the financial sector, mainly among building societies and life assurance businesses. The firm set up to run the UK rail network after the collapse of Railtrack PLC, Network Rail is a not for profit organisation. Network Rail is a company limited by guarantee which means that while they operate as a commercial business they have no shareholders but instead the board of directors is accountable to members who include passenger user groups and the train operating companies. Royal Mail Group, which includes the Post Office, is structured as a PLC but it is wholly owned by the government. **Co-operatives**, which can be worker owned or customer owned (the retail Co-op), have the potential to offer a sense of belonging and unity of purpose to the owners which is not found in conventional private sector firms.

The benefits of size

Economic theory predicts that large firms are likely to enjoy significant cost advantages due to economies of scale (see Figure 2.1 and Unit 4). The large firm operates further along its long run average cost (LRAC) curve than a small firm (e.g. Point B as opposed to Point A). The calculation of short and long run costs is covered in Unit 4.

Figure 2.1: Long run costs

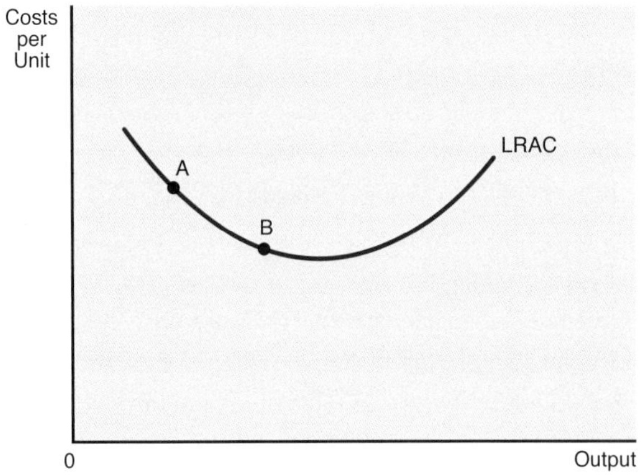

The small firm

The definition of a small firm depends largely on one's purpose; for example, if we are concerned mainly with small firms as employers, then numbers employed is important. According to the Bolton Report (1971) small firms have three distinguishing features: holding a relatively small share of the market; being managed by their owners in a personalised way, and not through any formalised management structure; not being part of any larger enterprise, so that owner-managers are free from any form of outside control. Small firms are usually sole traders, partnerships or private limited companies.

Continued existence of small firms can be accounted for by the following factors:

1. The minimum efficient scale of production (the level of output at which long run average costs are minimised) is low in many industries, thus there is little or no cost disadvantage to being small. There are no significant economies of scale for such firms as they have low fixed costs, e.g. small independent plumbers, decorators, electricians, etc.

2. Some specialist or niche markets exist that large companies do not wish to supply: Consider the demand for non-standard forms of production (e.g. in some forms of engineering and construction) or the irregular opening hours of corner shops, for instance.

3. The value placed upon personal attention in some areas, especially the service industries or the repair of products such as washing machines with parts and advice, e.g. management consultants. The convenience of small corner shops is another factor.

4. Contracting out. Many small firms supply larger companies.

5. Co-operatives. Independent businesses may join together to gain the advantages of bulk-buying while still retaining their independence. A good example is the UK grocery chain SPAR. In the UK there are 2,600 SPAR stores which turnover £2.6 billion in retail sales a year. Many workers co-operatives are small firms.

6. Monopoly power. Large firms may choose to allow smaller firms to exist in order to disguise restrictive practices (see Unit 15).

7. Some firms often remain small because they are unable to raise the finance that would enable them to expand.

8. Many family businesses remain small as they wish to remain in control of their business and don't want to take the risk of expansion.

The growth of firms

There are two sources of growth. **Internal growth** refers to a straight-forward increase in a firm's output scale of production; **external growth** occurs through merger with, or acquisition of, another company (see Unit 3). Motivation for growth may take one of the following forms:

1. A larger company may be able to exploit economies of scale more fully.

2. A larger company will enjoy a greater degree of market power, and will therefore be better able to exploit its market.

3. If the increase in size implies more product diversity, the company may be better able to withstand downturns in the economic cycle.

Growth, however, sometimes brings disadvantages:

1. The potential for suffering from diseconomies of scale (see Unit 4).

2. The inability to pay customers personal attention.

3. Some companies may expand too fast as did Sock Shop in the 1980's and find that they have insufficient **working capital** to cope with the extra commitments of a larger firm such as higher interest payments and more creditors. Expansion will increase a firm's financial commitments and with insufficient working capital it can simply run out of cash. Business tends to call this problem **overtrading** and many firms have learnt to their cost that cash and profit are not the same thing and many profitable firms have gone out of business because they have run out of cash. Cobra Beer expanded rapidly in recent years but failed to budget for a profit and was hit badly by the credit crunch in 2008. After going into administration Cobra was bought by Molson Coors in 2009.

Question 2.1

Research how the following help small firms:

(i)   Enterprise Finance Guarantee Scheme;   (iii) R&D tax credits;

(ii) The Prince's Trust;   (iv) National Loan Guarantee Scheme.

Question 2.2

Investigate the success of small breweries such as the Rebellion Beer Company.
http://www.rebellionbeer.co.uk/

Unit 3: **Forms of growth**

Types of growth

The growth of firms can be classified in terms of two categories. Internal growth refers to a firm becoming larger by expanding in its current market or finding new markets. Easyjet is a good example of a firm that has largely grown internally. External growth refers to the integration (joining together) of two formerly separate firms. Integration can take the form of a voluntary merger or a contested takeover.

Types of integration

Horizontal: Integration between firms at the same stage of production or distribution. The merger of the ITV companies Carlton and Granada in 2003 to form ITV created a national broadcasting entity, which had once been a number of regional television companies. Although names like Meridian, Central and Anglia survive ITV is now fully horizontally integrated. The changing nature of television such as the emergence of digital broadcasting and the competition from cable and satellite channels made such a merger logical. The only concern expressed by the competition authorities (Office of Fair Trading) over this merger was the enormous selling power ITV would have when it came to selling advertising time as it remains the biggest terrestrial commercial broadcaster in the UK. In the same vein the 2005 takeover of the cable company Telewest by its rival NTL is horizontal integration that is likely to be seen as being in the public interest (the company is now known as Virgin Media). The new company cemented the fragmented cable network providers into one firm; a strong rival to BT and BSkyB. In the summer of 2005 HMV, the retail group which owns the bookseller Waterstones showed an interest in buying a fierce rival of the latter, Ottakers. The retail book market would then be highly concentrated with 25% of the market controlled by the merged company. Both authors and publishers expressed concern that such a merger would not be in the public interest and invited the competition authorities to investigate. In the autumn of 2005 the Office of Fair Trading (OFT) referred the horizontal acquisition of HP Foods (owned by the French company Danone) by HJ Heinz to the Competition Commission. The OFT felt that the ownership of so many brands of soup and sauces (Lee & Perrins/Daddies) by one firm could lead to higher prices.

Significant horizontal mergers in recent years include the expansion of Banco Santander by purchasing Abbey National in 2004 and the savings accounts of the Bradford and Bingley Building Society and Alliance and Leicester during the credit crunch in 2008. Other notable horizontal mergers have been the supermarket takeover when Morrison's bought Safeway in 2003. More controversial was the takeover by Lloyds TSB of HBOS in 2008 which was brokered by the government during the 2008 banking crisis. In normal circumstances the OFT would never have allowed the merger due to competition issues and the 40% market share of the combined group but in that particular case the national interest was seen as more important than the public interest.

More recent horizontal mergers have been Virgin Active buying Esporta gyms in 2011 and also the planned purchase of the airline BMI by International Airlines Group which owns British Airways and Iberia.

Vertical: Integration between firms at different stages of production or distribution. If the firm taken over is at the next stage of the production or distribution process (e.g. a brewery buying a chain of pubs), then the integration is known as **forward-vertical**. A brewery buying a hops farm, on the other hand, is an example of **backward-vertical** integration. Vertical integration is common in the media (see the article at the end of the Unit). News Corporation owns 20th Century Fox and the latter's film library provides a source for the many movie channels operated by Sky and other TV channels owned by the company. Since 2004 Sony now own MGM which has 4,000 films in its library. Sony can use these films for video on

A brewery buying a chain of pubs is forward-vertical integration.

demand and new cable channels. While the latter are examples of backward vertical integration some businesses are fully vertically integrated forwards and backwards. For example BP as well as refining crude oil into petrol is also engaged in oil exploration and distribution of petrol at its filling stations. In October 2005 the Indian firm Apeejay Surrendra Group bought Typhoo tea from Premier Foods for £80m. Apeejay Surrendra grow a lot of tea in their Indian plantations, and buying Typhoo who blend and package tea should result in the benefits of forward vertical integration. The possible sale of Stansted Airport by British Airports Authority (BAA) could invite bids from airlines that pay landing charges to owners of airports such as BAA. If airlines such as Ryanair own airports this would be an example of backward vertical integration.

Conglomerate: Integration between firms that are in different, unrelated industries. These firms are said to be diversified. Conglomerate mergers are less common than they were in the 1960's and 1970's. Many large diversified conglomerates that grew through acquisition have been slimmed down in recent years to concentrate on core activities. For example Lonrho, which was once a huge conglomerate, was demerged in 1998 into Lonrho (focusing on hotels, property and distribution) and Lonmin, a mining company. In addition Hanson Trust split into four separate companies in 1996 (see the section on demergers). GUS (Great Universal Stores) was referred to as a conglomerate by the City when Burberry demerged from it in 2005 but GUS is focused only on retail and financial services, and is not as diversified as the famous conglomerates of the 1970's and 80's. The era of the great industrial conglomerate seemed to have disappeared in the new century but the Indian giant Tata Group is a good modern day example. It operates in 80 countries and is involved in seven different sectors which include steel, tea, hotels, construction and cars (it owns Jaguar and Land Rover).

Lateral: Integration between firms that are in different but related industries. The acquisition of Gillette by Procter and Gamble in 2004 is a good example of a lateral merger of two firms selling household consumer goods. Procter and Gamble is the biggest brands company owning Daz, Bold, Crest, Max Factor and Pampers. Gillette, apart from razors, owns Duracell batteries, Oral-B toothbrushes and Right Guard deodorant. In 2008 the Mars takeover of Wrigley was also a lateral merger with chocolate and chewing gum both being in the confectionery market. In 2010 the Kraft takeover of Cadbury was an example of a

lateral merger as both companies made a variety of similar products in the food and drinks sector. Lateral mergers can be particularly beneficial in that they provide opportunities for **economies of scope** (see Unit 4).

In recent years it has become popular for firms to co-operate in **alliances** and **joint ventures**. In the airline industry Star Alliance and One World are two groups of airlines which are integrated worldwide as air transport networks. Globalisation, increased airline competition and changes in passenger demands for air travel have meant that a single airline cannot sustain and respond alone to these changes. Similarly Airbus, a firm technically known as EADS, is owned jointly by European aircraft manufacturers is a realistic co-operative venture by Europe as a challenge to Boeing in the US. Airbus has been a very successful competitor to Boeing in the passenger airliner market with the rivalry reaching such an intensity that a major row broke out in 2005 when both Boeing and Airbus accused each other of receiving unfair levels of subsidies from their respective governments. Such joint activities by firms give them many of the advantages of a merger, particularly those linked to economies of scale, without them losing their separate legal identity.

Market concentration

The extent to which a small group of firms controls a given percentage of output or sales can be measured by the use of a **concentration ratio**. A simple concentration measure for a particular industry could be a '4 firm concentration ratio of 85%'. This means that the four largest firms in an industry account for 85% of the total output. Horizontal mergers tend to increase market concentration. Markets with a high level of concentration often give increased market power to the largest firms with some control over price. Highly concentrated markets are often called **oligopolies** (see Unit 10).

The data below refers to the market shares of the major film studios. There is a four firm concentration ratio of 61% because the four largest firms account for 61% of sales. An alternative measure of market concentration is the **Herfindahl Index**. It is often seen as more accurate than the simple concentration ratio because it considers all the firms in a market rather than just the largest. The index is calculated by squaring the percentage market share of each firm in the market and summing these numbers. The index can be as high as 10,000 for a pure monopoly with a 100% market share to as little as 10 or less for perfect competition.

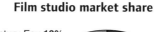

Film studio market share

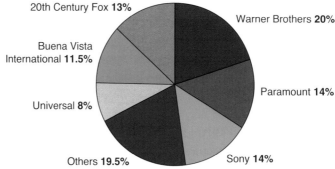

20th Century Fox **13%**
Buena Vista International **11.5%**
Universal **8%**
Others **19.5%**
Warner Brothers **20%**
Paramount **14%**
Sony **14%**

Some markets have a fairly low level of concentration, for example women's clothing. According to a report by Verdict Research in 2007 the top 10 retailers in womens' wear accounted for 51.5% of the market in 2007, compared with 41.5% a decade ago. The market is very competitive and in recent years traditional mass market retailers such as C&A and Littlewoods have been replaced by more dynamic value-led retailers including Primark, Matalan and TK Maxx.

The implications of growth

External growth has a number of attractions for the firm:

1. Rapid growth and acquisition of market power. Integration offers possibilities of increased market share and acquisition of valuable brand names. In recent years it has become common for a sum representing the value of a brand name to be included as an asset in the balance sheets of firms, even though this is an intangible asset. Acquiring brand names and market share through integration may prove cheaper, and is certainly quicker, than the alternative of internal growth.

2. Economies of scale. Expansion of output in the case of horizontal integration offers potential for lower long run average costs from a wide range of sources (technical, managerial, commercial, financial and risk-bearing economies of scale). For example the horizontal mergers that have produced Glaxo SmithKline Beecham (GSK) has given the firm significant research economies of scale in the pharmaceuticals sector. In the case of vertical integration, cost savings are made through cutting out profit margins at intermediate stages of production. A brewery, for example, that purchased a hops farm would now receive cheaper supplies of that particular ingredient and have greater control over quality of inputs.

3. Diversification. Conglomerate and lateral integration take firms into different product areas, making them better able to withstand a slump in any one market, while horizontal integration can give more geographical or brand diversification.

Integration is not always a success, however. The potential for **diseconomies of scale** should be considered and many of the mergers of the 1980s proved unsuccessful as measured by post merger profitability, with the profit made by the new, larger company falling short of the combined profits of the previously separate firms. More recently in the supermarket sector when Morrisons took over Safeway there was not perfect synergy as management and financial cultures differed between the two firms. However, there is a strong chance of long term success. Some companies have resorted to demerging in order to improve performance. One of the best recent examples of a failed merger was Daimler-Chrysler. Daimler-Benz bought Chrysler for $36bn in 1998 but the 'marriage' never worked chiefly because the cultures of the two car manufacturing firms were so different at management level. After nine years Daimler sold Chrysler to Cerberus, a private equity group. Dieter Zetsche, a senior Daimler executive, said of the ill-fated merger, "we overestimated the potential of synergies".

From an economy's point of view, integration is often regarded as detrimental:

1. It can confer a degree of **monopoly power**, which the neo-classical structure-conduct-performance model (see Unit 8) suggests will lead to the exploitation of the consumer.

2. Post merger rationalisation often leads to a direct loss of jobs (the Leeds-Halifax merger in 1995, for example, resulted in the closure of some branches, particularly where the two societies had branches in close proximity). Similar job losses are likely following the emergency banking mergers of 2008 as a result of the credit crunch. In June 2009 Lloyds announced the closure of its Cheltenham and Gloucester Building Society branches.

3. Research by the economist Geoffrey Meeks found that two-thirds of mergers in the United States reduced shareholder value.

Despite this, integration can sometimes receive government encouragement, because domestic firms may need to be large to compete internationally. However, internal growth is generally held in more favourable regard than external growth. This is especially so when it entails product innovation. Marks and Spencer and more recently Virgin have grown through internal growth whereas easyJet has grown by both internal and external growth. EasyJet has grown in size in the low cost airline market by its own success and by taking over one of its rivals, the British Airways subsidiary, 'Go', some years ago.

The trend towards demerger

Since the 1990's a trend towards the break-up of larger companies began to emerge. It appeared that difficulties inherent in managing large firms, particularly conglomerates, were being recognised and that many companies saw the benefits in becoming 'more focused' on particular lines of business. Typical of this trend were the selling off of some Forte assets after the group had been taken over by Granada and the splitting of the Hanson conglomerate into four separate firms announced in February 1996. In the same month, British Gas announced that it would split into two companies, one responsible for the maintenance of the pipe network (Transco) and the other for gas supply (Centrica). This move was made in response to the forthcoming removal of the company's monopoly over domestic gas supply. ICI demerged part of its group into Zeneca in 1993, and in 2001 BT demerged into BT Group and O_2. It is possible that failed mergers can subsequently lead to demergers. A more recent demerger in April 2003 was that of hotel, pub and restaurant group Six Continents (formerly Bass). Cadbury grew over the years as a food and drinks business but in more recent years changed direction. With the disposal of Schweppes and Dr. Pepper in 2007, Cadbury focussed on its confectionery – mainly chocolate.

The Chairman at the time, Sir John Sunderland, praised the Cadbury Schweppes' demerger into confectionery and beverages in March 2007:

> "We believe now is the moment to separate and give both management teams the focused opportunity to extract the full potential inherent in these excellent businesses."

However, in 2009 Cadbury itself was controversially taken over by the US food giant Kraft and then in 2011 the enlarged company was demerged with Kraft chairman and chief executive Irene Rosenfeld justifying the plan to split up as follows:

> "Our strategic actions have put us in a position to create two great companies, each with the leadership, resources and strong market positions to realize their full potential."

The main motives for demergers focus on several issues. Sometimes the problems of **diseconomies of scale** – mainly managerial – are the main factor. In addition changes in market conditions are important with the result that the firm reassesses its strategic direction. Technological change can also play a part with new markets developing and others declining. The demerger of Cable and Wireless in 2010 was motivated in part by the explosive demand for telecoms bandwidth across the globe. Clearly pressures from shareholders, who are always looking for increases in shareholder value, are also an important factor in decisions on whether to demerge. This quote from Cable and Wireless plc illustrates this point:

> "In November 2009, Cable and Wireless plc announced its intention to separate Communications and Worldwide, reflecting the Board's belief that the two businesses had reached a position where they are best placed to deliver further value to shareholders as separately listed companies."

Kraft demerger announced:

Kraft Foods Inc today announced that its Board of Directors intends to create two independent public companies: A high-growth global snacks business with estimated revenue of approximately $32 billion and a high-margin North American grocery business with estimated revenue of approximately $16 billion. The company expects to create these companies through a tax-free spin-off of the North American grocery business to Kraft Foods shareholders.

"As our second quarter results once again show, our businesses are benefiting from a virtuous cycle of growth and investment, which we fully expect will continue," said Chairman and CEO Irene Rosenfeld. "We have built two strong, but distinct, portfolios. Our strategic actions have put us in a position to create two great companies, each with the leadership, resources and strong market positions to realize their full potential. The next phase of our development recognizes the distinct priorities within our portfolio. The global snacks business has tremendous opportunities for growth as consumer demand for snacks increases around the world. The North American grocery business has a remarkable set of iconic brands, industry-leading margins, and the clear ability to generate significant cash flow."

Strategic rationale

Over the last several years, Kraft Foods has transformed its portfolio by expanding geographically and by building its presence in the fast-growing snacking category. A series of strategic acquisitions, notably of LU biscuits from Danone and of Cadbury Plc, together with the strong organic growth of its Power Brands, have made Kraft Foods the world's leading snacks company. At the same time, the company has continued to invest in product quality, marketing and innovation behind its iconic North American brands, while implementing a series of cost management initiatives. As a result, the company has delivered strong results in very challenging economic conditions.

Having successfully executed its transformation plan, and 18 months into the Cadbury integration, the company has, in fact, built a global snacking platform and a North American grocery business that now differ in their future strategic priorities, growth profiles and operational focus. For example, Kraft Foods' snacks business is focused largely on capitalising on global consumer snacking trends, building its strength in fast-growing developing markets and in instant consumption channels; the North American grocery business is investing to grow revenue in line with its categories in traditional grocery channels through product innovation and world-class marketing, while driving superior margins and cash flows.

Over the course of Kraft Foods' strategic transformation, the Board of Directors and management have continually explored opportunities to further enhance performance and increase long-term shareholder value and believe that creating two independent public companies is the logical next step. Specifically, detailed review by the Board and management has shown that these two businesses would now benefit from being run independently of each other, rather than as part of the same company.

The company believes that creating two public companies would offer a number of opportunities:

● Each business would focus on its distinct strategic priorities, with financial targets that best fit its own markets and unique opportunities.

● Each would be able to allocate resources and deploy capital in a manner consistent with its strategic priorities in order to optimise total returns to shareholders.

● Investors would be able to value the two companies based on their particular operational and financial characteristics and thus invest accordingly.

Creating two great companies

Global snacks will consist of the current Kraft Foods Europe and Developing Markets units as well as the North American snacks and confectionery businesses. As an independent company, global snacks would have estimated revenues of approximately $32 billion and a strong growth profile across numerous fast-growing, attractive markets. Approximately 75% of revenues would be from snacks around the world, and approximately 42% would come from developing markets, including a diversified presence in numerous highly attractive emerging markets. The business would have a strong presence in the fast-growing and high-margin instant consumption channel. The non-snacks portion of the portfolio would consist primarily of powdered beverages and coffee, which have a strong growth and margin profile in developing markets and Europe. Key brands would include *Oreo* and *LU biscuits*, *Cadbury* and *Milka* chocolates, *Trident* gum, *Jacobs* coffee, and *Tang* powdered beverages.

The North American grocery business would consist of the current US Beverages, Cheese, Convenient Meals and Grocery segments and the non-snack categories in Canada and Food Service. With approximately $16 billion in estimated revenue, this business would be one of the largest food and beverage companies in North America. Its portfolio would include many of the most popular food brands on the continent, with leadership positions in virtually every category in which it competes.

The North American grocery business would have a highly competitive retail presence, cost leadership and a continued commitment to innovation and marketing excellence. North America's strategic priorities would be to build on its leading market positions by growing in line with its categories while maintaining a sharp focus on its cost structure. Capitalising on the investments that the company has made during its transformation, an independent North American business would be managed to deliver reliable revenue growth; strong margins and free cash flow; and a highly competitive dividend payout. Key brands would include *Kraft* macaroni and cheese, *Oscar Mayer* meats, *Philadelphia* cream cheese, *Maxwell House* coffee, *Capri Sun* beverages, *Jell-O* desserts and *Miracle Whip* salad dressing.

Grocery Company	**Snack Company**
Kraft Cheese (Dairylea)	Cadbury (Dairy Milk)
Philadelphia Cheese	Milka
Maxwell House	Oreo
Capri Sun	Lu
Jello-O	Trident
Oscar Meyer	Tang
Miracle Whip	Jacobs

Source: Kraft Foods website; http://www.kraftfoodscompany.com

Question 3.1

In 2007 Thomas Cook Group took over My Travel creating a huge holiday giant. The merger will result in job losses with the closure of 150 of the combined group's travel agencies plus My Travel's headquarters in Rochdale. Indeed the North-West of England will suffer the worst of the job losses in customer support and telephone bookings. My Travel's airline operations at Manchester Airport will close down with the combined aircraft fleet operating as Thomas Cook Airlines. In total up to 2,800 jobs may go in the UK as a result of the merger.

In 2011 the company had to ask for help from its banks having been hit hard by tough trading conditions, especially in Britain. There its core customer base of families with young children was particularly affected by tough economic conditions. It has also been hit by political unrest in popular destinations such as Egypt, Tunisia and to a lesser extent Morocco.

Question: Using the above information examine the cost savings that can be made as a result of horizontal integration.

Question 3.2

Demerger survival

Peter Bartram, Financial Director, 26 April 2007

Demergers are a massive undertaking, definitely not for the faint-hearted Finance Director (FD). But done properly they can improve business focus and create long-term value. Bryan Hucker, finance director of Coda, the accounting software supplier, still bears the scars of the company's 2006 demerger from AIM-listed CodaSciSys.

"I was talking to analysts recently," he recalls. "I told them that if an FD tells them they've been through a demerger and knows everything about it, ask them one question: would you like to do another. Those who really understand it will be the ones heading for the door before you've even finished speaking."

He adds, "It was a massive exercise, beyond the understanding of anyone who has never done it." Yet, if the trend towards demergers continues to grow, more FDs could find themselves wanting to head for the door.

"Normally, you find demergers follow on after waves of substantial and sustained merger and acquisition activity," says Dr Duncan Angwin an associate professor in the strategic management group at Warwick Business School. "Sometimes, companies expand beyond their ability to control and co-ordinate. Then, perhaps, they find that they're not realising the benefits they originally anticipated," he says.

According to Thomson Financial, there were €1.35 trillion of mergers and acquisitions in Europe last year. So, if Angwin is right, FDs should brace themselves for the demerger fall-out in the next few years. Demergers have grabbed the headlines in recent weeks because of Cadbury Schweppes's stated intention to separate its confectionery and American beverages businesses. According to chief executive Todd Stitzer, the move will enable the demerged companies "to focus on generating further revenue growth, increasing margin and enhancing returns for their respective share owners."

As Stitzer and his management team have set out a reasonably convincing strategic rationale for the demerger, he may well be right. New research suggests that companies that demerge to improve business focus as well as communication with investors are more likely to create value in the long run.

Question: What are the potential advantages and disadvantages of demergers?

Source: Financial Director

Question 3.3

Why we'll not see the likes of the barnstorming James Hanson again.

Today's conglomerates are to be found in private equity, not the publicly quoted sector.

In the heady days of the 1980's, when Thatcherism was at its most potent and companies everywhere seemingly trembled at the prospect of who would be taken over next, business was dominated by buccaneering larger than life characters who bestrode the corporate stage. Lord James Hanson, Tiny Rowland and Hector Laing were big names associated with conglomerates such as Hanson, Lonrho, and Imperial Group. These conglomerates were extensively diversified with Hanson producing anything from bricks to batteries and Tompkins was often referred to as the 'buns to guns combo'.

These business empires and their bosses have long gone in the 21st century. They will never return, at least not in the form of quoted stock market companies (PLC's) with shareholders to keep happy and corporate governance rulebooks to abide by. Hanson, a group that spanned chemicals, bricks, coal and electricity as well as tobacco was split into four parts in 1996. As for Lonrho, once the owner of everything from hotels to the Observer newspaper, it has been reduced to a shadow of its former self in the name of Lonmin, a platinum producer.

Why will these conglomerates not return in their original form as quoted companies? One reason is that the word 'conglomerate' has long been a term of abuse in the City. The buzzword now is 'focus'. Investors are no longer interested in, or trusting of, companies which house an array of completely different businesses under one roof. They demand managements who understand the individual businesses they run, not financial engineers, for whom coalmines are no different from widget factories provided the same philosophy of squeezing cost and sweating capital is employed.

The other reason is governance. These days, it would simply be impossible to run a publicly-quoted conglomerate as a private fiefdom in the way that, say, Lonrho was controlled by a chief executive who famously likened his non-executive directors to 'decorations on a Christmas tree'. In truth, nor would the boards of Hanson and Lord Weinstock's GEC – another conglomerate run by a long-gone titan of industry – have borne much scrutiny in today's climate, packed as they were by timeservers and insiders and relatives.

However, the conglomerate is not entirely dead. Rather, it has emerged in another form known as the private equity firm – funds, which operate well away from the glare of public scrutiny. They are also run, by and large, by faceless accountants although there are some odd and honourable exceptions – Philip Green, the owner of Bhs and Arcadia, Guy Hands of Terra Firma, and Robin Saunders, the former diva from WestLB, to name but three. Think of what takeover activity there is today and consider how much of the action revolves around private equity bids. Will Sainsbury's get taken out?

So, where we once had Hanson and Hutchings and Rudd and Rowland, here is the face of capitalism, 2004-style: Cinven, CVC Partners, Permira, Duke Street Capital, and Bridgepoint. These are the nearest you will get to a conglomerate these days – vulture funds that gobble up quoted companies (PLCs), chew the fat from them and then spit the remains out to be served up once more by ordinary investors. CVC, for instance, is the owner of William Hill, the AA, Halfords, Kwik-Fit, Debenhams, and IG Index – a rag-bag of disparate businesses if ever there was – while Bridgeport includes Adams Childrenswear, Virgin Active and Holmes Place. Permira is the owner of Travelodge and Premiere.

Does any of this matter? In a way it does, because large swathes of corporate Britain are not accountable to shareholders as would be the case with a PLC. Away from the glare of public scrutiny these organisations are free from rowdy shareholders at the AGM where the small investor or the pressure group can embarrass board members in full view of the national media. Compared to the heady days of the 1980's the conglomerate has become a different commercial entity and some would argue that it makes the business world a duller place.

Source: Michael Harrison, *The Independent*, 3/11/04 (adapted)

Essay: Evaluate the view that producers gain and consumers lose as a result of the integration of firms.

Question 3.4

What type of integration were the following mergers: Asda/Walmart, Daimler-Chrysler, Air France-KLM.

Question 3.5

The history of Santander in the UK

Since its entry into the UK market in November 2004, Santander has transformed the three businesses it acquired. The integration of separate management structures, systems and brands improved profitability and allowed Santander to broaden its range of value-for-money products which contributed to strong organic growth.

Key dates for Santander in the UK include:

● In November 2004, the courts approved Santander acquisition of Abbey National plc and Abbey became part of the Santander Group.

● In September 2008, Santander acquired Bradford & Bingley's retail branches and savings business.

● In October 2008, Santander acquired Alliance & Leicester. In January 2010, Abbey and the branch network of Bradford & Bingley rebranded as Santander.

● In August 2010, Santander agreed to purchase the parts of the banking businesses of the Royal Bank of Scotland which are carried out through its RBS branches in England and Wales, and by its NatWest branches in Scotland.

● In November 2010, Alliance & Leicester was rebranded as Santander.

Source: http://www.aboutsantander.co.uk

Question: How could Santander benefit from these acquisitions?

Short run costs

Economists distinguish between two different time periods – the short-run and the long-run – when considering costs of production. The **short-run** is defined as a period in which the enterprise has decided its 'scale of plant' (or 'capacity size') and thus can only increase output by increasing the use of that fixed capacity and by acquiring the use of additional variable factors of production, e.g. labour, raw materials. There is at least one fixed factor of production. Thus, the enterprise has some fixed costs that cannot be avoided (even if the firm stopped production) and some variable costs which are avoidable, i.e. they are directly related to output, and could be avoided if the firm closed down. Therefore, to produce any given level of output, the enterprise incurs fixed and variable costs. The fixed costs would not vary as output varies (e.g. rent, interest charges on borrowed capital, business rates and certain administration costs). Variable costs would be items such as wages (labour), raw material costs, heating, lighting, power, fuel and transport costs because they rise in total as output rises.

For any level of output, there are thus several measures of cost – this is why the expression 'cost of production' is ambiguous. Examples of costs are:

Total cost of production = Fixed costs + Variable costs

Average total cost (or per unit cost) (sometimes called 'average cost') = $\dfrac{\text{Total cost}}{\text{Output}}$

Marginal cost = The addition to total cost of producing one more unit of output

Average fixed costs = $\dfrac{\text{Total fixed cost}}{\text{Output}}$

Average variable costs = $\dfrac{\text{Total variable costs}}{\text{Output}}$

Figure 4.1: Costs in the short run

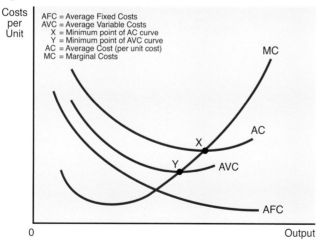

The relationship between marginal cost and average cost is essentially mathematical. If marginal cost is less than average cost, average cost is falling because the average is being pulled down. Similarly if marginal cost is greater than average cost, average cost is rising because the average is being pulled up. It is best explained in cricketing terms. When a batsman's next (marginal) innings is less than his present average the result is that the average is pulled down. The reverse occurs when the next innings is above the current average.

The marginal cost curve will therefore normally intersect the average variable cost and average cost curves from below at their lowest point.

It is important to remember that even if marginal cost is falling total costs will still be rising as long as marginal cost is positive. The basis of costs in the short-run rests on the **law of increasing/diminishing returns** to a variable factor of production, usually labour. The shapes of the marginal cost and average variable cost curves are based on increasing returns (falling marginal and average variable costs) and diminishing returns (rising marginal and average variable costs). The average cost curve will fall when both average fixed cost and average variable cost are falling, but it will rise when the fall in average fixed cost is less than the rise in average variable cost.

Diminishing returns should not be confused with diseconomies of scale, which is a long run concept. The diminishing returns theory relates to the additional returns (output) that result from marginal increases in a variable factor of production (e.g. labour) when it is combined with some other fixed factor of production (e.g. land or capital), which is fixed. It is essentially a relationship between input factors in the short-run whereas returns to scale is a concept which analyses what happens when all factor inputs rise.

For example, suppose additional workers (labour) are added to a fixed plot of land. Although (initially) marginal output (i.e. extra output) may increase because of teamwork; ultimately, as more and more workers are added to the fixed plot, the marginal additions will begin to diminish. The scope for increasing output when capital and land are fixed falls. In this context, if marginal returns (or product) are changing, so will average returns (or average product). Taking the example of additional workers applied to a given plot of land, one worker working the plot can produce a total output of 5 tonnes of potatoes. Two workers working the plot can produce a total of 15 tonnes of potatoes, because (a) more of the plot can be cultivated, i.e. the fixed factor is being more effectively utilised and, (b) two workers are likely to be more efficient, working as a team and dividing the work load. If the total output of the two workers is 15 tonnes, the **marginal product** (or return) of the second worker must be 10 (tonnes), i.e. his addition to total output. **Average product** rises from 5.0 to 7.5. It is not that the second worker is more efficient than the first, simply that the two workers make better use of the fixed factor. As more workers are added, total output will rise but, ultimately, the fixed factor (the plot of land) will become overworked. In this case, the marginal product (returns) of additional workers will start to diminish. Total output increases, but each time by smaller and smaller amounts. Figure 4.2 illustrates these situations and is derived from the table below.

Column 1 Number of Workers	Column 2 Fixed Factor Land	Column 3 Total Output of Potatoes	Column 4 Marginal Return (or product) of Labour	Column 5 (= Col. 3 ÷ Col. 1) Average Return (or product) of Labour
1	1	5	5	5.0
2	1	15	10	7.5
3	1	27	12	9.0
4	1	32	5	8.0
5	1	36	4	7.2
6	1	38	2	6.3
7	1	38	0	5.4

In the example, the maximum average return to labour (maximum output per worker) is achieved when three workers are applied to the fixed factor. This is referred to as the **optimum factor combination** (of fixed and variable factors). In this case, it is 1:3. It represents the best combination of fixed and variable factors in terms of output per worker, but note the total output of 32 may not be the most profitable level of output. This will depend on sales and the price of potatoes in the market. The marginal product/average product curves tell us little about profitable levels of production. The average product and marginal product curves help to determine the average cost and marginal cost curves for a firm in the short run. The relationship between the four is shown below in Figure 4.3.

Figure 4.2: Short-run returns to labour

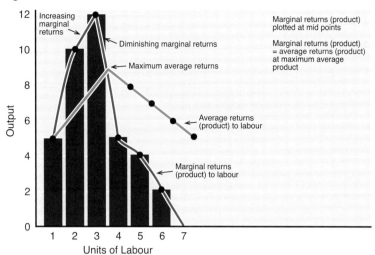

Figure 4.3: Relationship between cost and product curves

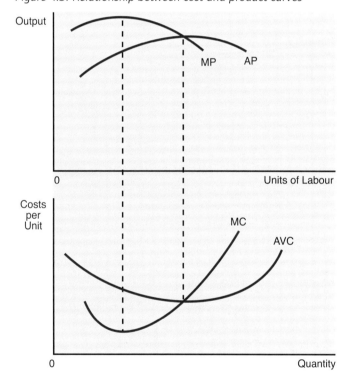

Marginal product cuts average product at its maximum point. The minimum point on the marginal cost curve is associated with the highest point on the marginal product curve. The minimum point on the average variable curve is associated with the highest point on the average product curve.

Long run costs

The long-run is defined as a period when the enterprise can alter its scale of plant (either expand or contract size). All factors of production thus become variable. It is likely that, as the scale of plant increases, the enterprise may enjoy the benefits of internal economies of scale. Where these are achieved, the average total cost in the long-run (LRAC) is likely to fall. This is shown in Figure 4.4.

Points A, B, C, represent points on the long-run average total cost curve. Note these do not necessarily correspond to the minimum point on each short-run average cost curve (SRAC), e.g. point X. All points on

the long-run average cost curve (LRAC) show the least cost or minimum attainable average cost of production for any given output, assuming the firm is able to adjust its scale of plant accordingly. In the basic micro-economic theory of the firm, the assumption is that firms will always choose the least-cost method of production in the long-run and hence move out along the LRAC curve if this is possible, (lack of finance or lack of demand may prevent the firm from moving along this curve as it would like to do). It is important to remember that increasing and diminishing returns to a variable factor (e.g. labour) is the most important factor affecting the AC, AVC, and MC in the short-run. Equally the long-run average cost curve is strongly affected by economies and diseconomies of scale.

Figure 4.4: Costs in the long run

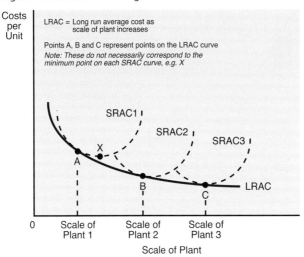

When an increase in the input of all factors of production leads to a *more than proportional* increase in output, we say that the firm has experienced **increasing returns to scale**. For example, if the firm increases the scale of production, that is the input of all factors of production, by 10 per cent, and as a result output rises by more than 10 per cent, the firm has experienced economies of scale resulting from a rise in productivity. On the other hand, when an increase in the input of all factors of production leads to a *less than proportional* increase in total output, we say that the firm experiences **decreasing returns to scale**. Thus if the firm increases the scale of production by 10 per cent and output rises by less than 10 per cent, then we say that the firm has experienced decreasing returns to scale.

If a firm is experiencing economies of scale then the LRAC will be falling, whereas diseconomies of scale will lead to rising LRAC. If a 10% rise in inputs leads to a 10% rise in output then a firm is experiencing constant returns to scale and the LRAC will be constant. Increasing returns to scale are thus a source of economies of scale.

Figure 4.5: Returns to scale

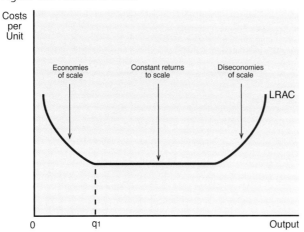

The output level of 0q1 in Figure 4.5 represents the **minimum efficient scale (MES)**, which produces the lowest average cost of production in the long run. The points of MES vary considerably between firms and this explains why some industries comprise many small firms while others include a few large firms. MES is the level of output beyond which average costs fall no further. The shape of the long term average cost curve will vary from industry to industry, and also over time due to technological change.

Sources of economies of scale

Technical economies

These result in increases in productivity, arising from the process of production when the scale of a firm's operations increases. There are three key technical economies of scale.

(i) **Specialisation:** The bigger the firm the greater the opportunities for increased specialisation. Specialist machinery will allow the firm to increase capital and labour productivity (total factor productivity) thus lowering long run average costs.

(ii) **Indivisibilities:** A firm will always be able to increase its productivity by using more efficient capital. For example, if two machines perform exactly the same task, but one machine produces three times as much per hour than the other productivity will be increased by using it. However, capital equipment with high levels of productivity is often large and expensive needing a high throughput. In many cases it is indivisible in the sense that it is not available in a smaller version. Assembly lines for mass-produced cars, nuclear power stations and oil refineries are examples of large pieces of capital equipment which cannot be scaled down below a certain level of production. Only when a firm's output grows will it be able to afford to use these large pieces of capital equipment; at low levels of output these indivisible units of capital equipment would be under-utilised and the firm would be operating with excess capacity.

(iii) **Linkage of processes (multiples):** Products often need a number of separate processes to produce a finished item. If the first machine in a production process has a capacity of 20 units per hour and the second machine has a capacity of 15 units per hour the firm will require an output of a least 60 units per hour to use all its machinery to its full capacity and maximise productivity (3 of the first machine and 4 of the second) This assumes only a two stage production process. Thus the larger the level of output the more efficient is the linkage of processes because a firm with an output of 40 units would have capacity under-utilised in the second stage of production.

Marketing economies

Large firms gain from the benefits of bulk purchase because they are powerful enough to buy raw materials and other inputs at a discount. They can often demand huge discounts from their suppliers by threatening to take their business elsewhere using their huge buying power as a threat. This has often been alleged of supermarkets in the UK who have been accused of demanding such large discounts from suppliers such as farmers and meat processors that the latter are unable to make even minimal levels of profit. This has been particularly true of dairy farmers.

Firms, which are large, can use their own lorry fleets and bulk containers to transport goods to markets. The scale of the method of transport used means that cost per unit transported falls for firms using bulk transportation methods such as supertankers for oil. In addition large firms are able to buy advertising time on TV and radio with discounts from broadcasters. The same principle can apply to the purchase of advertising space in newspapers and magazines.

Financial economies

Large firms are often able to obtain finance more cheaply and easily than smaller firms as they have a higher credit rating. Banks may consider them to be a lower risk than smaller firms partly because of a

more established reputation and also because they can offer more collateral security. Accordingly large firms can often obtain more favourable repayment terms and lower rates of interest than smaller firms; hence lowering costs per unit.

Managerial economies

Once a firm becomes larger it can employ specialist managers and departments to deal with key functional areas such as marketing, finance, sales and purchasing. The expertise of specialist personnel can help to make the organisation run more efficiently at a higher level of productivity and hence a lower unit cost.

Research economies of scale

Large firms have the resources to commit themselves to major research programmes in search of new products. To be a successful global car producer firms need to be large. MG Rover failed in part because it was not large enough to command the research resources to develop new cars to replace its ageing models. It could not compete globally with the likes of Toyota, Nissan and Ford. It was said that MG Rover was "too small to be big and too large to be small". This meant that it was too small to develop, produce and sell new cars for the global car market but too large to be a niche producer such as Morgan, TVR and Bristol Cars. Similarly large pharmaceutical firms such as GSK, Astra Zeneca and Pfister have the resources to take research risks with many ideas in the development of major new drugs in medical science some of which may never reach the market. The latter point is often called **risk-bearing economies of scale**.

Diseconomies of scale

It is possible that beyond a certain level of output further increases in the scale of production might lead to diseconomies of scale. The suggestion is that large firms can eventually become more difficult to manage. This can be because of problems organising and coordinating the firm's activities resulting in slow and ineffective decision-making and poor communication. Diseconomies of scale chiefly result from the managerial side of the business and can result in the firm splitting itself into separate operating divisions or even demerging.

External economies of scale

The above analysis of economies of scale only deals with **internal economies of scale**, so called because they arise from within the firm itself. There are also external economies of scale which arise from changes within the whole industry and which benefit all firms within that industry, whatever their size. A technological breakthrough may reduce the costs per unit of all the firms in an industry, shifting the long run average cost curve downwards at all levels of output (see Figure 4.6).

Figure 4.6

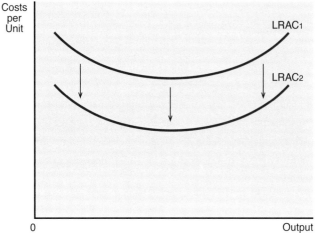

Another important external economy relates to the concentration of an industry in a particular geographical area. In the UK car manufacture was traditionally concentrated in the Midlands, textiles in Lancashire and shipbuilding in the North-East. There are now new examples of what is called **external economies of concentration**. 'Silicon Fen' is the name given to the region around Cambridge, which is home to a large cluster of high technology knowledge based businesses which focus on software, electronics and biotechnology. This growth has obviously been developed thanks to links with the university, and there have been suggestions that a motorway link between Oxford and Cambridge would expand this further creating a 'brain belt' between the two old university towns.

Similarly there has been the growth of a cluster of high tech firms linked to Formula 1 racing in the motor sport industry in Northamptonshire and Oxfordshire. The use of Silverstone in Northamptonshire for the British Grand Prix has obviously been a factor in the growth of this industry in the UK. According to the Motorsport Industry Association; "The companies found within this motorsport cluster provide engineering solutions and act as a global centre for the production of performance cars. A supporting services industry offering specialised legal, financial and insurance services has also built up around these world-class design and manufacturing businesses." When a number of firms making the same product locate close together the local labour force is geared up to the skill requirements of the industry. Local colleges often run courses geared to employment in the industry and specialist support firms are attracted to the area to provide parts or specialist services. Local government may improve transport links in the area. When a whole area is geared to the needs of one industry which commands a lot of the employment, the benefits of lower costs feed through to all firms. The strength of the Lancashire textile industry in the early part of the last century owed much to external economies of scale.

However, it is possible that if too many firms from the same industry locate in one area local labour becomes scarce and firms have to offer higher wages to attract new workers, often poaching them from rival firms. Land and factory space can become scarce and rents begin to rise. Local roads become congested and so transport costs begin to rise. These problems are called **external diseconomies of scale**. Most seriously if the whole industry goes into decline as a result of falling demand for its products then the whole region in which it is located will suffer very high **structural unemployment**. This happened with Lancashire textiles and the shipyards on the Tyne and the Clyde when cheaper imports made it impossible for UK firms to compete.

Economies of scope

When a firm increases the number of different goods it produces, long run average costs of production can fall. Economies of scope refer to efficiencies associated with the range of products available from a firm. Take, for example, a firm such as Procter and Gamble which produces a huge range of products not directly related to one another, from razors to toothpaste. They can afford to hire expensive graphic designers and marketing experts, who can use their skills across many different product lines. As the firm's management structure, design, marketing, administrative systems and distribution costs are spread over such a large product range this lowers the average cost of production for each product.

Revenue

Revenue for a firm is calculated by multiplying price by quantity demanded.

$\therefore$ **Total Revenue** = Price x Quantity

In Figure 4.7 Op_1 x Oq_1 = Total Revenue. This is the shown as the coloured rectangle.

If Total Revenue (TR) is divided by quantity (Q) then the result is Average Revenue (AR)

$\therefore AR = \dfrac{TR}{Q}$

Figure 4.7: Total and average revenue

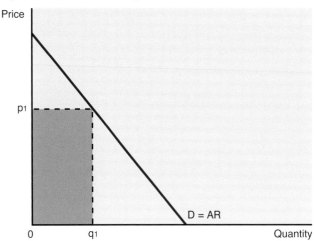

Also: $AR = \dfrac{TR}{Q} = \dfrac{P \times Q}{Q} = P$

Thus **Average Revenue** (AR) also equals price, which means that the demand curve is also the average revenue curve.

Marginal Revenue (MR) is the addition to Total Revenue as a result of selling one more unit, which once calculated, can be shown on a diagram.

Price (£)	Quantity Demanded	TR	AR	MR
10	1	£10	£10	
9	2	£18	£9	£8 = £18 - £10
8	3	£24	£8	£6 = £24 - £18
7	4	£28	£7	£4 = £28 - £24
6	5	£30	£6	£2 = £30 - £28
5	6	£30	£5	£0 = £30 - £30
4	7	£28	£4	£-2 = £28 - £30
3	8	£24	£3	£-4 = £24 - £28
2	9	£18	£2	£-6 = £18 - £24
1	10	£10	£1	£-8 = £10 - £18
0	11	£0	£0	£-10 = £0 - £10

The Marginal Revenue (MR) line shown in Figure 4.8 is at first positive and then negative. Where MR = 0 the firm will maximise its sales revenue. Each time average revenue falls by £1 marginal revenue falls by £2 and thus the gradient of MR is twice as steep as AR.

It is important to remember that the price elasticity of demand varies along the length of the demand curve. Over the full price range demand is perfectly elastic at the price axis and perfectly inelastic at the quantity axis. At points on the demand curve above X demand is progressively more price elastic whereas below point X demand is progressively more price inelastic. The point marked X is at the mid-point on the demand curve and also indicates unit elastic demand (price elasticity of demand = (-)1). If price is above p1 then a fall in price will raise sales revenue because MR is positive (demand is price elastic). If price falls to below p1 sales revenue will fall because MR is negative (demand is price inelastic). When MR = 0 at point X then total revenue is maximised as shown in the diagram.

Figure 4.8: Marginal, average and total revenue

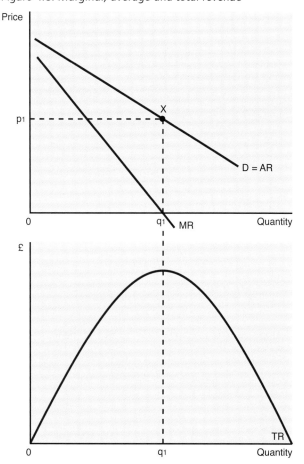

Question 4.1

You are given the following information:

Cost per tonne of fertiliser = £140; Fixed cost of land = £3000; (Assume that no further costs are incurred.)

Selling price of wheat = £2 per unit.

Tonnes of fertiliser applied to a fixed area of land	Total production (units)
0	1000
1	1100
2	1250
3	1500
4	1900
5	2150
6	2275
7	2350
8	2380
9	2330

(a) With reference to the above data, comment on the relationship between the application of fertiliser and the production of wheat.

(b) What level of fertiliser would a profit maximising farmer choose to apply? Show the amount of wheat produced and the profit earned. Justify your answer.

Source: ULEAC, Economics Paper 3, June 1983

Question 4.2

Given below are the cost and price data for a profit maximising firm.

Output Level per Period	Total Variable Costs (£)	Total Fixed Costs (£)
1	5	5
2	9	5
3	12	5
4	16	5
5	22	5
6	31	5
7	34	5
8	52	5
9	76	5
10	107	5

(a) Assume that the market price is constant at £18 per unit. At what level of output would profits be maximised?

(b) If the market price were to decline from £18, at what prices would the firm cease production (i) in the long run and (ii) immediately? (See Unit 7.)

Source: ULEAC, Economics Paper 3, June 1981

Question 4.3

Using the concept of price elasticity of demand to explain why price P_1 in Figure 4.8 will maximise sales revenue for the firm.

Question 4.4

When MG Rover cars went out of business in 2005 it was argued that they were too small to be big and too big to be small. Explain what this might mean.

Question 4.5

Using the diagram below, explain what is meant by internal economies and internal diseconomies of scale.

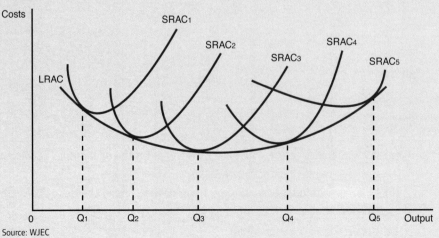

Source: WJEC

Unit 5: **The behaviour of the profit maximising firm**

Short run profit maximisation

Neo-classical economic theory assumes that firms aim to maximise profit, which is defined as the difference between revenue and cost. The point should be reinforced that by 'cost' economists mean the opportunity cost of the factors of production and that economic cost thus includes an allowance for normal profit (the level of profit which is just sufficient to keep the factors of production in their present use). The difference between revenue and cost is thus **supernormal/abnormal profit**.

Marginal analysis is commonly used to determine the profit maximising level of output for a firm. Figure 5.1 shows a firm facing a downward sloping demand curve, left to right. This tells us the price at which the firm will be able to sell a given number of units during a given period of time. The demand curve is the firm's average revenue curve too, because the price of the product is the revenue that will be gained from each unit of it sold. If the firm wishes to sell more of its product, it must reduce the price on *all* units of the good sold. The extra (marginal) revenue from the sale of one more unit is thus less than the average revenue (price). From a mathematical point of view the marginal revenue curve (MR) is twice as steep as the average revenue curve (AR).

Figure 5.1: Profit maximisation

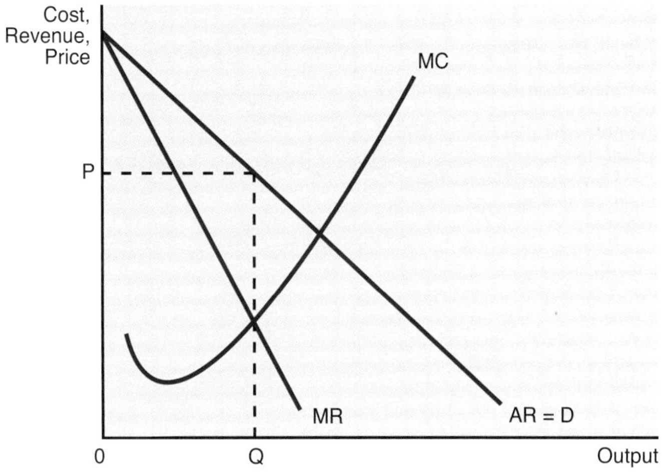

The profit maximising level of output is shown in the diagram as Q, and occurs where marginal cost (MC) is equal to marginal revenue (MR):

$$MC = MR$$

For proof, take any point to the left of Q. Here, MR exceeds MC, so producing an extra unit must add to profit. For a point to the right of Q, MC exceeds MR, so producing an extra unit will decrease profit. It is thus worth expanding output to Q but not beyond. Price level P is associated with the profit maximising level of output level Q. It is important to remember that the **marginal profit** is zero on the last unit produced (at Q in the above diagram). This is because the cost of producing the last unit (the marginal cost) is equal to the revenue from selling it (the marginal revenue).

Long run profit maximisation

The neo-classical assumption takes a short term view of profit maximising, in as much as it implies that a firm will adjust its price and output rapidly in response to changes in market conditions. However, if

Increased competition from new entrants often forces firms to cut margins or reduce costs.

consumers dislike price changes, it may be the case that long run profit levels will be enhanced by the maintenance of a stable price. Thus it is possible that price will only be changed when it becomes clear that a change in market conditions will persist into the long run. This is particularly so where a firm pursues a mark-up pricing policy (price = cost of production plus a percentage mark-up known as **cost-plus pricing**). The cost-plus approach to pricing involves calculating all the costs associated with producing and marketing a product on a per unit basis and then adding a margin to provide a profit. The profit per unit can be expressed as a percentage of the cost, in which case it is referred to as the **mark-up** or sometimes as a **mark-on**.

$$\text{Mark-up} = \frac{\text{Selling Price} - \text{Cost Price}}{\text{Cost Price}} \times \frac{100}{1}$$

$$\text{Mark-on} = \frac{\text{Selling Price} - \text{Cost Price}}{\text{Selling Price}} \times \frac{100}{1}$$

The only thing that will change the price charged is then a long run shift in cost conditions or possibly a change in market conditions. A severe recession or increased competition from new entrants often forces firms to cut their margins or find ways to reduce their costs. Long term profit maximising might entail forward-looking policies that would be rejected by a company more interested in short term profit levels. Unit 17 examines the issues associated with 'short termism'.

Question 5.1

If the price a profit-maximising firm can sell its output is fixed by the government it will produce at a level of output where

(a) average cost is equal to average revenue.

(b) average cost is minimised.

(c) marginal cost is equal to price.

(d) total revenue is maximised.

(e) total cost is minimised.

Unit 6: **Alternative goals for the firm**

The question as to the objectives that a firm will set itself is a complex one, and the standard neo-classical profit maximising assumption is regarded by many as too simplistic however important profit might be to a firm (see Unit 1). Other possible goals include:

Revenue maximisation

Figure 6.1 highlights the fact that a sales revenue maximising firm will expand output until MR is zero. This is because while MR is positive, each extra unit sold adds to revenue. Selling extra units beyond the point where MR is zero would, on the other hand, reduce revenue. The firm's output is thus Qsr and the price charged Psr, which contrasts with neo-classical profit maximising output of Qpm and price Ppm. If a firm pursues sales revenue maximisation it's likely to have a bigger share of the market than if it profit-maximised.

Figure 6.1: Sales revenue maximisation

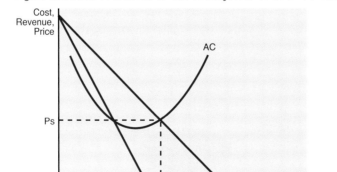

Ppm = Price to maximise profit
Psr = Price to maximise sales revenue

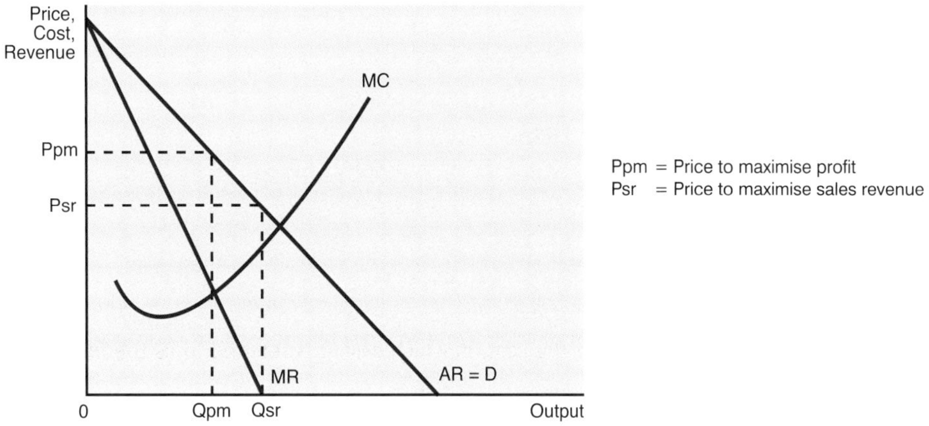

Sales maximisation

A firm might wish to maximise the number of units sold, in turn maximising its share of the market, although this goal would have to be pursued subject to a profit constraint. The firm could expect to sell a large number of units if it dropped its price far enough, but at some point cutting price any further will involve making a loss. Figure 6.2 shows the output and price of a firm, which wishes to maximise sales subject to the constraint of making at least normal profit. Output is thus set at the level where AR = AC because if price fell below Ps with output above Qs then AR<AC and losses would be made.

Figure 6.2: Sales volume maximisation subject to constraint of normal profit

The divorce of ownership and control

Other theories result from debate about who is in control of the firm. Shareholders own the firm and are likely to want it to maximise profits for their dividends, but they have little direct input as to how the company should be run on a day-to-day basis. This is in the hands of a board of directors who may have other objectives in addition to making profits. Thus ownership of the company is divorced from control. This illustrates the **principal-agent problem** where the manager (the agent) does not always act in the best interests of the shareholders (the principal). It is important to establish where control of the company lies because the behaviour of the firm will largely be determined by this factor. It is worth noting that in recent years there has been an increase in the popularity of private limited companies whose affairs are not open to the same scrutiny as is the case with public limited companies (PLCs). Virgin Group and Arcadia, which includes British Home Stores, are private companies. Decision-making on key strategic objectives by the board of directors of a PLC is likely to be subject to more constraints than in a private limited company. A PLC's shares can be traded openly on the Stock Exchange and shares can thus be bought by anyone who then has rights to attend the Annual General Meeting and question board members. In recent years pressure groups such as Greenpeace have bought shares in PLCs who may have not, in their view, been taking enough care with environmental issues. These pressure groups may not be able to exert real power but they can articulate their viewpoints effectively. Most recently individual shareholders have used the AGM of PLCs to complain about directors' bonuses.

Managerial theories of the firm

When a firm introduces sales revenue maximisation or growth in market share as objectives as seen above this often illustrates the divorce between ownership and control in large organisations. Managerial theories are based on the assumption that managers control the company. Managers may have their own agenda, and wish to pursue goals such as maximising their own prestige or even simply enjoying an easy life. Sometimes perks and status are not tied directly to profit maximisation and thus managers make enough profit to prevent a shareholder revolt, while still enjoying the perks afforded by not striving to maximise profits.

Behavioural theories

American economist Herbert Simon argued that decision-making within a company is the result of interaction between many competing groups within the firm. The rank and file workers might have different goals to those of the sales manager, for example, and the objectives of the sales manager are likely to be different to those of the production manager, and so on. The behaviour of the firm will then depend upon the balance of power between these competing groups. Reconciling the various competing groups within large organisations with many levels of management involves a decision making process from which emerges '**satisficing**'. Bargaining among managers will produce compromises which can be seen as satisfactory – hence the term satisficing. Minimum targets may be set for a range of objectives such as market share or sales turnover. This can carry on until more difficult trading conditions occur, then managers will remove organisational slack (**X-inefficiency**) in the firm by possibly reforming work practices and announcing redundancies for example.

Other goals

The special nature of an organisation might dictate its goals. Consider, for instance, the values that inspire worker-cooperatives or a company that is set up for charitable purposes. Many firms are now aware that they need to satisfy, as far as is possible, all the **stakeholders** of the firm, i.e. customers, employees, shareholders, lenders etc. Stakeholders are people who have an interest in the activities of a firm. In particular industries objectives unique to that sector are obviously important. In the airline sector a key objective is the 'load factor' on each flight i.e. the percentage of seats filled. Airlines may be aiming for an 85% load factor for example. Load factors are important in businesses such as air travel where most of the costs are fixed. Network Rail probably places more emphasis on safety and maintenance than its more profit-motivated predecessor, Railtrack. In addition ethical and environmental objectives have become more important to firms operating in sensitive areas of production such as oil and chemicals. It is common for large firms to produce an annual social audit of their activities which examines the positive and negative effects of the firm's operations on the wider society.

Question 6.1

Many firms aspire to broader objectives than merely profit maximisation as seen below with British Petroleum (BP).

BP Group Values

What we do

We deliver energy to the world.

We find, develop and produce essential sources of energy. We turn these sources into products that people need everywhere.

The world needs energy and this need is growing. This energy will be in many forms. It is, and will always be, vital for people and progress everywhere.

We expect to be held to high standards in what we do. We strive to be a safety leader in our industry, a world-class operator, a good corporate citizen and a great employer. We are BP.

What we stand for

We care deeply about how we deliver energy to the world.

Above everything, that starts with safety and excellence in our operations. This is fundamental to our success.

Our approach is built on respect, being consistent and having the courage to do the right thing. We believe success comes from the energy of our people. We have a determination to learn and to do things better. We depend upon developing and deploying the best technology, and building long-lasting relationships.

We are committed to making a real difference in providing the energy the world needs today, and in the changing world of tomorrow. We work as one team. We are BP.

Safety

Safety is good business. Everything we do relies upon the safety of our workforce and the communities around us. We care about the safe management of the environment. We are committed to safely delivering energy to the world.

Respect

We respect the world in which we operate. It begins with compliance with laws and regulations. We hold ourselves to the highest ethical standards and behave in ways that earn the trust of others.

We depend on the relationships we have and respect each other and those we work with. We value diversity of people and thought. We care about the consequences of our decisions, large and small, on those around us.

Excellence

We are in a hazardous business and are committed to excellence through the systematic and disciplined management of our operations. We follow and uphold the rules and standards we set for our company. We commit to quality outcomes, have a thirst to learn and to improve. If something is not right, we correct it.

Courage

What we do is rarely easy. Achieving the best outcomes often requires the courage to face difficulty, to speak up and stand by what we believe. We always strive to do the right thing. We explore new ways of thinking and are unafraid to ask for help. We are honest with ourselves and actively seek feedback from others. We aim for an enduring legacy, despite the short-term priorities of our world.

One Team

Whatever the strength of the individual, we will accomplish more together. We put the team ahead of our personal success and commit to building its capability. We trust each other to deliver on our respective obligations.

Source: British Petroleum.

Question: To what extent do the values set out above conflict with profit maximisation?

Question 6.2

A publisher has to decide the price at which to sell a new book. He estimates that the costs incurred before publication amount to £10,000 and that variable costs amount to £1 a copy. In addition, he has agreed to pay the author royalties at a rate of 10 per cent of sales revenue. The publisher's best estimate of the number of books he would sell at different prices is as follows:

Price (£)	Number Sold
1.00	60,000
1.25	40,000
1.50	35,000
1.75	20,000
2.00	10,000

(a) Which of the above prices would maximise the publisher's profits?

(b) Which of the above prices would maximise the author's royalties?

Source: ULEAC, Economics p3, June 1977

The above model has had great significance over the last sixty years when examining markets. The structure-conduct-performance analysis can be shown in a diagram as set out below.

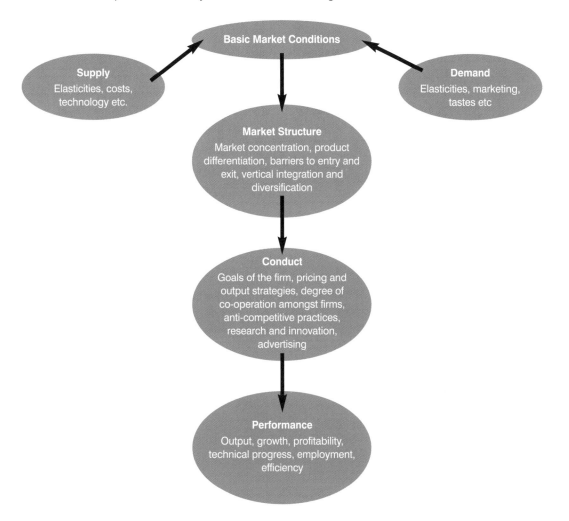

Basic market conditions (demand and supply) determine the structure of a market (either competitive or monopolistic), which in turn will determine conduct (such as pricing) and performance (such as profitability). The implication is that markets, which are highly concentrated such as monopolies, are able to set high prices or engage in anti-competitive practices, which result in abnormal profits and efficiency losses. The structure-conduct-performance can give competition authorities a valuable reference point for firms and industries, which may be acting anti-competitively.

In recent years the structure-conduct-performance model has been criticised, specifically by the contestable market approach developed by William Baumol. His view was that it did not matter whether an industry was highly concentrated (dominated by a few firms) as long as firms were free to enter and leave the market without making losses. A **contestable market** is one where there are low entry and exit barriers and no sunk costs. A **sunk cost** is one which cannot be recovered when a firm leaves an industry such as advertising and research expenditure. This view suggests that government intervention to control monopolies and mergers should be based on a policy, which examines the contestability of the market as well as its structure. This and other issues raised here are developed in the forthcoming units.

Unit 7: **Perfect competition**

Market characteristics:

1. Many buyers and many sellers.

2. All firms and consumers enjoy perfect knowledge of market conditions.

3. Homogeneous (identical) products.

4. Complete freedom of entry to, and exit from, the market in the long run (there are no barriers to entry; since cost advantages constitute a barrier to entry, this implies that all firms have identical cost structures). Such a market is thus perfectly contestable.

Conditions 1-3 combine to render each firm a **price taker**: Small in relation to the market and producing a product identical to that of many other firms, the firm has to accept the market price. Any attempt to raise prices will lead to complete substitution away from the firm's product, given the perfect knowledge enjoyed by consumers. As a price taker, the firm can sell as much as it wishes at the going market price, that is to say it is faced by a perfectly elastic demand curve. This results in a constant average revenue (AR) and marginal revenue (MR), but how much the firm will sell is subject to the constraints of its cost curves. The perfect knowledge of firms in this type of market means that there is no incentive for technological change as any idea or process introduced by one firm would immediately be available to all the others. Thus there would be no way for a firm to recover its research costs.

Short run equilibrium

Figure 7.1 shows the industry equilibrium on the left hand side. The right hand side illustrates the situation facing each individual firm operating in the market. They accept the price determined at industry level and then supply the quantity of output that will maximise the firm's profits. In the short run, it is possible that market conditions will permit individual firms to make supernormal profits, as represented by the shaded area in the diagram (the excess of AR over AC multiplied by output). It is important to note that the profit maximising level of output of the firm Q_F is not at minimum average cost in the short run.

Figure 7.1: Short run equilibrium under perfect competition

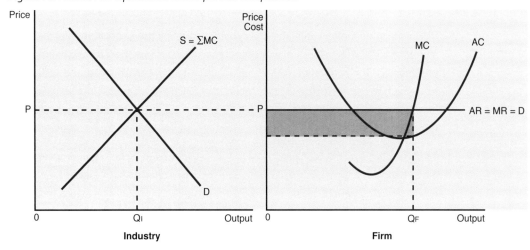

Long run equilibrium

Freedom of entry ensures that only normal profit will be made in the long run, as any short term supernormal profits will attract new firms into the market and erode profits. As new firms enter, the industry's supply curve shifts to the right (S→S1) lowering the market price (P→P1). Figure 7.2 depicts the long run equilibrium position. Note that were losses to be experienced in the short run, the long run would see firms leaving the industry and the price rising to restore long run equilibrium. Firms will continue to enter or leave the industry until normal profits are made, at which point there is no further incentive to enter or leave the industry.

Figure 7.2: Long run equilibrium under perfect competition

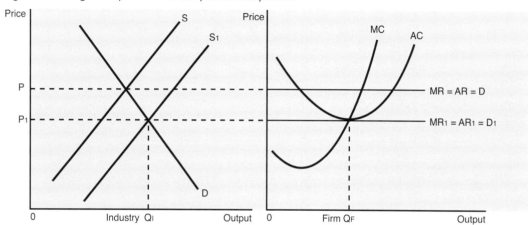

The firm's supply curve

The fact that MR is equal to price for the firm operating under conditions of perfect competition, combined with the MR = MC profit maximising condition, allows us to find the output level of the firm at any given price simply by reading across from that price to the MC curve. In other words, the firm's MC curve is its supply curve, as highlighted in Figure 7.3.

Figure 7.3: Construction of the firm's supply curve

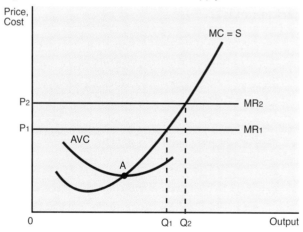

One point of qualification is required here. If the market price is not sufficient for the firm to cover its variable costs, then the firm faces a bigger loss by continuing to operate than by closing down and continuing to pay fixed costs (until the relevant contracts expire). The firm's supply curve is therefore the section of its MC curve rising above its average variable cost (AVC) curve, and point A on the diagram above is known as the '**shut down point**'. In the long run, the firm will close if it cannot cover average total cost (P = AC). A firm is thus required to at least make normal profits in the long run.

The industry's supply curve is derived by the horizontal summation of the supply curves of all the individual firms operating in the market.

Question 7.1

Consider the accompanying graph, and then answer the questions.

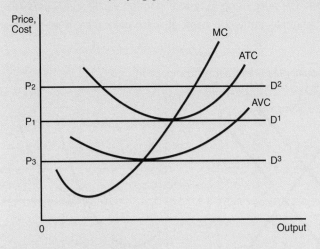

(a) Which demand curve indicates that the firm is earning normal profits?

(b) Which demand curve indicates that the firm is earning abnormal profits?

(c) Which demand curve indicates that the firm is indifferent between shutting down and producing?

(d) Which curve is the firm's supply curve?

(e) Below which price will the firm shut down?

(f) Which position would see firms wanting to enter this industry?

Do perfectly competitive markets exist?

The model explained in this unit is a theoretical abstract. That is to say that no real world industry possesses all of the characteristics of the perfectly competitive market structure.

The model remains a useful analytical tool, however, for by estimating how close a market is to being perfectly competitive, we can predict how closely the behaviour of the market will conform to the predictions of the model. Given that perfectly competitive markets produce desirable outcomes (see Unit 12) the model also presents an ideal at which to aim. This can be useful for the Competition Authorities such as the Office of Fair Trading.

Some markets that approximate to perfect competition are those for agricultural produce, foreign currency exchange and buying and selling shares on the Stock Exchange. In the agricultural sector small-scale dairy farmers produce a homogeneous product (milk). There are many sellers and the firms are price takers as they have no control over price individually. In the foreign exchange market there are many dealers in currencies, which are homogeneous. Each 100 Euro note looks the same to a buyer, and dealers in currency do not individually affect the exchange rate.

Summary

Perfect Competition

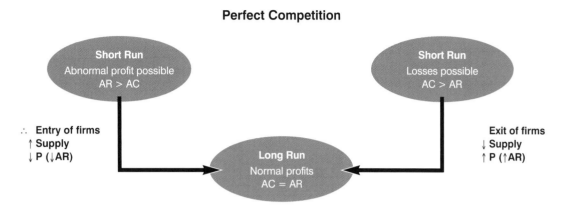

Perfect competition results in a productively and allocatively efficient market (see Unit 12). Perfectly competitive markets are also **X-efficient**. This means that the market produces a given output with the fewest possible inputs, which implies that better outcomes are not possible. All points on the cost curve (including the productively-efficient point where the average cost is lowest) are X-efficient.

Question 7.2

Investigate the view that the growth of e-commerce has introduced some of the characteristics of perfect competition to many markets.

Question 7.3

Study the diagram below, which shows losses being made in a perfectly competitive industry in the short run. Explain how the industry will reach long run equilibrium from this position.

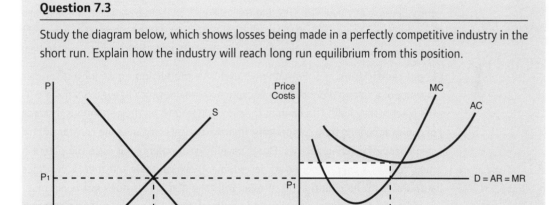

Unit 8: **Monopoly**

Of the market structures recognised by neo-classical theory, monopoly lies at the opposite end of the spectrum from perfect competition. By definition, a monopolistic market is one in which only one seller operates. From a legal point of view, however, monopoly is taken to exist wherever one firm (or a cartel, a number of firms acting in collusion) enjoys a market share in excess of 25 per cent (see Unit 15). Such a definition is required because a market share of this magnitude may be sufficient to confer substantial control over prices. Good examples of monopolies in the UK are the water companies such as Thames Water who are a **pure monopoly** to domestic customers in geographical areas. Pure monopolies have a 100% market share.

Market characteristics

1. Only one firm

2. High enough barriers to entry to prohibit new entry in both the short run and long run
These **barriers to entry** take one or more of a number of forms:

(a) **Capital costs and expertise.** e.g. firms find it hard to break into the oil business because large amounts of expertise are needed to compete with existing oil companies.

(b) **Economies of scale.** In some industries economies of scale are very large. This will act as a barrier to entry because any new firm entering the market is likely to be small in the first instance and therefore have higher average costs than existing producers. In natural monopolies (see Unit 12) economies of scale are so great that it is unprofitable for more than one firm to exist in an industry.

(c) **Legal restrictions.** e.g. Patents give exclusive production rights for a given period of time to the inventor of a certain product. Pharmaceutical companies such as GlaxoSmithKline (GSK) rely heavily on the patents they hold. This enables them to gain returns on their enormous research costs without fear of copies appearing from competitors. Pharmaceutical companies are constantly challenged to stay one step ahead of expiring patents. Drugs have 20-year patents but once the patent has been registered there follows a lengthy period of development, clinical trials and then acceptance by the regulatory authorities in the country where sales will take place. This does not leave much time to reap the benefits of the monopoly protection from the patent. When drugs are on patent they are very costly for health authorities, but once the patent expires for a drug the patent holder's market share shrinks rapidly as other companies quickly offer cheaper generic alternatives. Astra Zeneca's Prilosec and GSK's Paxil both lost their patent protection in recent years. Pfizer's Viagra had patent protection until 2011 and was a major revenue source for the firm. The huge cost of developing groundbreaking drugs has led to mergers and acquisitions in the pharmaceutical industry in recent years as they seek the benefits of **research economies of scale**. In 1990 the market share of the top ten pharmaceutical companies totalled 28%; by 2007 it had risen to over 40%. In the UK firms can register their intellectual property rights such as patents, designs, copyright and trade marks at the Intellectual Property Office. The Patents Act 1977 gives patents a maximum 20 year life although other firms can produce a patented product under licence which involves paying royalties to the patent holder. If a firm has been granted patent, it must renew it every year after the 5th year for up to 20 years protection. Some would argue that monopoly, like perfect competition, provides little incentive for research and innovation. However, monopolies often have sufficient profit to plough into research and the market power to reap the benefits from innovation, a view held by Schumpeter (dynamic efficiency).

The concept of a **Patent Box** has been the subject of a government consultation in recent years and legislation is now being introduced to apply from April 2013. The key feature of the legislation will be to allow companies to pay only a 10% rate of Corporation tax on all profits attributable to qualifying intellectual property. This will cover patents granted by the UK or the European Patent Office.

The full benefit of the regime will be phased in over the first four financial years from April 2013. In the first year the proportion of relevant profits to which the 10% rate will apply is 60% and this will then increase annually to 100% from April 2017. The Patent Box is designed to encourage firms to research and develop new products in the UK.

For many years Royal Mail had a legal monopoly over the letterpost but this has been eroded in recent years partly by technological change and partly by the liberalisation of the postal sector (see Question 8.4). Until the late 1980s only the state owned National Coal Board was legally allowed to mine for coal in the UK.

(d) **Control of a scarce resource or input.** e.g. The De Beers Syndicate in South Africa enjoyed sole access to what was almost the only land on which diamonds could be mined, although the syndicate's dominance has recently been threatened by new sources in Russia and Africa. Ownership of the sole supply of raw materials gives a producer a powerful weapon against possible entrants.

(e) If an existing firm has better information about the way the industry works than the potential new entrant it will take expensive time for new entrants to acquire this know-how. This **information imbalance** is a reality in many markets and a significant barrier to entry. The technical name for this is **information asymmetry**.

(f) **Advertising.** If existing firms spend heavily on advertising, new firms will have to do so as well, if they are to compete on equal terms. Advertising drives up average costs, but does build up brand loyalty.

(g) **Brand proliferation.** If existing firms provide a wide range of similar products but with slightly different characteristics, it will be harder for any new firm to find a niche in the market. In this way a three-firm concentration ratio (the percentage of the market supplied by the largest three firms) of around 90% has been achieved by Kellogg's, Weetabix and Nabisco (part of Kraft) in the cereal industry. See also entry limit pricing (Unit 11).

When examining entry barriers it is often convenient to split them into structural and behavioural barriers. **Structural barriers** are not deliberately erected by existing firms and are therefore quite innocent. Start-up costs and those relating to economies of scale would fall into that category. **Behavioural barriers** are erected by the firms to deliberately prevent the entry of a new firm and these may include limit pricing and refusal to allow access to a scarce raw material supply. The controversy over British Telecom allowing other internet suppliers access to the 'local loop' was a behavioural barrier to entry and investigated by the Competition Commission with a view to BT 'unbundling' it.

To ensure that rival telecom operators had equal and fair access to BT's local network Openreach was created in 2006 following an agreement between BT and the regulator Ofcomm. Openreach manages BT's local network which connects customers to their local telephone exchange. Although Openreach is owned by the BT group of companies, it is operated independently of the BT company

3. Exit barriers

In some industries there are significant costs for a firm to pay when it decides to leave an industry. These closure costs arise as a result of redundancies to workers, landscaping the site, meeting environmental clear-up costs, disposal of equipment, etc. Firms facing huge exit costs may decide to carry on operating in activities they might otherwise leave because of huge closure costs. The US Steel industry was originally in this position in the late 1990's as cheap imports poured into the USA. President Bush's tariffs on imported steel kept production going in many plants. The US steel industry has firms which are unable to

Entry and Exit barriers lead to a misallocation of resources because factors of production cannot move freely.

shut down inefficient plants. The price of closure is too high especially with redundancy costs, pension fund liabilities, health care liabilities, and environmental liabilities. Bethlehem Steel had a massive burden of legacy costs with 70,000 pensioners and 130,000 members of its healthcare plan. The long-term liability totalled almost $10bn. The costs of closure often thus exceed the cost of running the steel mills. After a decline in the US steel industry and management problems leading to the company's 2001 bankruptcy, Bethlehem Steel was dissolved and the remaining assets sold to International Steel Group (ISG) in 2003. In 2005, ISG merged with Mittal Steel, now known as ArcelorMittal.

Similar exit barriers resulting from high employee liabilities faced the troubled US car manufacturers, Ford, GM and Chrysler, in the recent recession. Exit barriers can act as an entry barrier because if firms know that it is difficult to leave an industry they will not try to enter it in the first place. Entry and exit barriers lead to a misallocation of resources because factors of production cannot move freely from one activity to another. It is important to remember that such costs act as both an exit and an entry barrier. Heavy expenditure on advertising, as it is non-recoverable on exit, acts as a significant exit barrier. Sunk costs are non-recoverable costs when a firm leaves an industry. These include start up costs such as marketing, research and development as well as exploration costs, which exist in both the oil and gas industry and mining.

Rather bizarrely governments can act directly to prevent the exit of a firm. In 2005 a French judge ordered the Swiss food giant Nestlé to re-open a loss making factory. Nestlé were told to re-launch production at the chocolate and Nescafé plant outside Marseilles which employed 427 workers. Nestlé called the ruling 'unbelievable and unprecedented' claiming that it abridged its basic freedom to manage its operations and that the loss-making plant would never become profitable. In the US the Chapter 11 bankruptcy law provides an opportunity for a firm to stay in an industry when its financial difficulties would suggest that it should leave. In late 2011 American Airlines' parent company AMR Corporation filed for Chapter 11 bankruptcy protection which refers to a section of the US Bankruptcy Code. It protects a company from its creditors, giving it time to reorganise its debts or sell parts of the business. Hence exit from the industry is delayed or even prevented. American Airlines' rivals Delta and United both filed under Chapter 11 post the 9/11 terrorist attacks but have since returned to profitability after having successfully restructured their labour contracts and cut costs.

Equilibrium

Given the market characteristics, the downward sloping market demand curve must also be the demand curve for the monopolist's product. Consequently, the monopolist has the power to be a **price-maker**: It can set the price. If it does this, it then sells whatever quantity consumers are willing to buy at that price. If the monopolist prefers instead to choose the quantity to sell, it must then accept the corresponding price. It is for this reason that the monopolist is said to be 'constrained by his demand curve'. The monopolist is assumed to be a profit maximiser which means using MC = MR to set output.

Any abnormal profits (the orange shaded area in Figure 8.1) that are made can persist into the long run, because of the high barriers to entry. Accordingly, the short and long run equilibria are identical, as shown below. It is important to note that the red shaded area represents total costs (average cost x output).

Figure 8.1: Price and output under monopoly

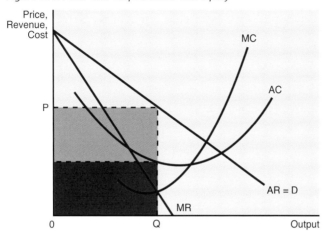

As the price charged by the monopolist is above its marginal cost it is said to be **allocatively inefficient**. In addition because output is below minimum average cost of production it is said to be **productively inefficient** (see Unit 12). Liëbenstein (1966) suggested that the allocative inefficiency of monopoly is likely to be less important than the internal inefficiency of '**X-inefficiency**'. As entry barriers protect a monopolist it is under little pressure to behave efficiently and minimise costs. Price can always be raised to maintain profits. Cutting costs involves unpopular and difficult decisions thus it is easier to keep this 'organisational slack' when a monopoly. How many firms with monopoly power have X-inefficiency? It could be argued that British Airways has had to tackle X-inefficiency since it lost its monopoly on certain routes and has had to face the competition from budget airlines. Some firms are often called **natural monopolies** which means that these firms minimise their long run average costs at a level of output which is close to the national level of demand. These monopolies are thus productively efficient and breaking them up to create competition simply results in several sub-optimal firms. Infrastructure businesses such as Network Rail (the rail system) and National Grid (electricity and gas) are natural monopolies.

In the diagram below (Figure 8.2) it is more efficient to have one firm producing 200 units than four competing firms producing 50 units.

Figure 8.2

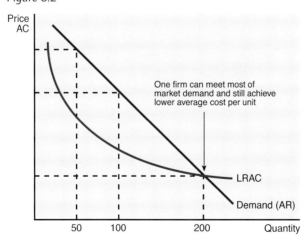

It can also be argued that monopoly can be a better outcome for a market than perfect competition as a result of the benefits of economies of scale enjoyed by a monopolist.

The diagram below (Figure 8.3) can be used to show the benefits of monopoly which arise from economies of scale. Assuming constant average costs the competitive firm has higher costs (LRACc) and its price is Pc. The monopolist operates with lower long run average costs (LRACm) and its price is Pm. Monopoly results in a higher price and a lower output which produces a welfare loss shown in red. However, there are significant cost savings resulting from the monopolist's economies of scale. These are shown as the green area and if this area is larger than the red area an industry is in theory better off being monopolised than competitive.

Figure 8.3

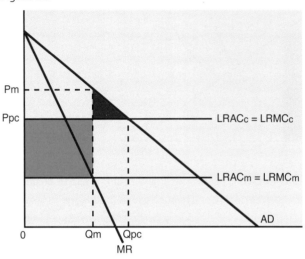

Price discrimination

Where market conditions permit, a monopolist might choose to price discriminate. This entails charging different prices to different groups of consumers for the same product or service. Firms with some degree of monopoly power have the ability to be price makers. If a single market price is charged, most purchasers of the product will enjoy consumer surplus. The term **consumer surplus** is used to represent the difference between the actual price paid by a consumer and the price they would have been willing to pay. For example, if I value a chocolate bar at 40p but purchase it for 25p, I enjoy 15p worth of consumer surplus. The area under the demand curve bounded by the vertical axis and the price line represents consumer surplus diagramatically. If the monopolist is able to raise the price above P (see Figure 8.4) to P_1 for some customers, then it is able to appropriate some of their consumer surplus in the form of extra monopoly profits.

Figure 8.4: Consumer surplus and price discrimination

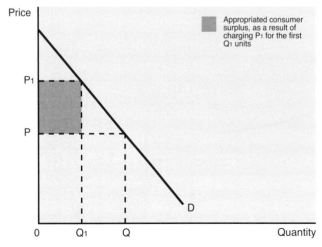

Perhaps the most important condition for price discrimination to be possible is that, after the market has been sub-divided, the sub-markets can be kept separate. Were it possible to buy the product in a low price sub-market and travel to a higher priced sub-market in order to re-sell at an intermediate price, price discrimination could not be effective. Time barriers, for example, keep markets for peak and off-peak travel separate; geographical barriers allow products to be sold for different prices in different countries. Markets can also be separated by age, charging less to pensioners and children than the standard price to adults. It is normal for each sub-market to have different price elasticities of demand with the highest prices being charged to the group of consumers with price inelastic demand and the lower prices to consumers with elastic demand. By raising the price to consumers with inelastic demand and lowering it to those with elastic demand revenue for the firm will rise.

First degree price discrimination

First degree price discrimination occurs when the producer charges each individual consumer the highest price they are prepared to pay. As a result the producer captures the entire consumer surplus, which then becomes extra producer revenue. In Figure 8.5 the producer is able to identify each potential consumer right up to the point where the price is so high no one will buy the product. It is difficult to find examples of this type of price discrimination although the Internet auction web site e-Bay has some similarities. A seller on e-Bay will capture the entire consumer surplus of the successful bidder if the auction is hotly contested. If for example a seller has five rare identical football programmes for sale on e-Bay and the auction is highly contested by say ten bidders then it is possible that the seller captures the entire consumer surplus of the five successful bidders. With this type of price discrimination the demand curve is actually the marginal revenue curve as in such an auction the price does not have to be lowered to sell additional units of the product.

Figure 8.5: First degree price discrimination

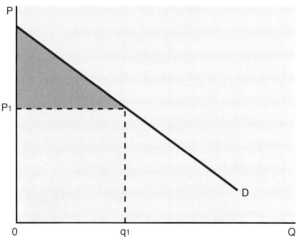

Second degree price discrimination

When a firm has surplus capacity it is possible that some potential consumers will be targeted by a lower price. These consumers would not normally buy the product at the standard price but a special lower price will attract them. This type of pricing is particularly popular when there is spare capacity and the low special price (marginal revenue) is higher than the marginal cost. Football stadiums in the lower divisions are often not filled to capacity and sometimes clubs introduce special offers for adults to bring children who only pay £1 to gain admission (often called 'kid a quid'). This kind of pricing adds to revenue but adds little to costs. As long as the special price is above marginal cost this type of pricing results in increased profits. In Figure 8.6 the shaded area represents the extra revenue from special lower prices.

Figure 8.6: Second degree price discrimination

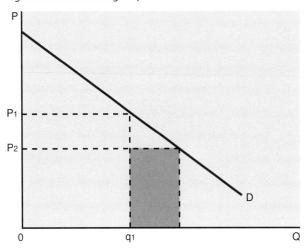

Third degree price discrimination

Figure 8.7 illustrates the process of maximising profit by distinguishing between two sub-markets. First, the monopolist determines his overall profit maximising output. The demand curve D_T is the total market demand curve, by implication the horizontal summation of the demand curves in the two sub-markets. Output (Q_T) is thus set at the level where the corresponding marginal revenue function (MR_T) is equal to marginal cost. The most profitable way to distribute this output between the two sub-markets is to do so in such a way that marginal revenue in the sub-markets is equated. To understand why, suppose marginal revenue were higher in sub-market A than sub-market B. By transferring a unit of output from sub-market B to sub-market A, more revenue would be gained than lost. Since the cost of production for one sub-market does not differ from production for the other, total cost remains unchanged and profits are increased. More units should be transferred until the marginal revenues are equal. Having decided on the appropriate output level for each sub-market, the price in each is determined by reading up to the relevant demand curve.

Figure 8.7: Third degree price discrimination

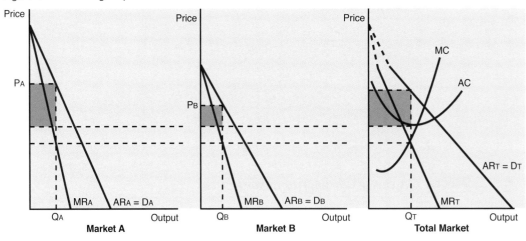

Note that if each sub-market had the same demand curve, the marginal revenue curves would be identical too, resulting in the same output and price level in each sub-market. Consequently, price discrimination can only be effective if the sub-markets have different demand curves. Demand elasticity must differ in each market. The firm will charge the higher price in the market where demand is less elastic, and thus less sensitive to price.

It is not necessary that price discrimination be limited to two sub-markets. The analysis above can be generalised to any number of sub-markets without affecting the conclusions. Indeed, if the firm could isolate each customer as a separate sub-market, it would charge each one just the price they were willing to pay, thereby appropriating the entire consumer surplus. This is known as perfect price discrimination or first degree price discrimination.

There are numerous examples of price discrimination from the real world. The most well known are associated with rail travel and telephone charges. Off-peak travel and phone calls are cheaper than at other times. This enables the producers to spread demand so that peak times are less congested. It does mean that peak time users with a more inelastic demand are possibly being over-charged.

Other examples include the main supermarkets charging more for some products in stores where their clientele is predominantly higher income and less in stores where shoppers are on lower incomes. British Airways has been accused of charging higher prices for a flight booked in the UK compared to someone booking the same flight overseas. Football fans have found that 'home' supporters are often charged less than 'away' fans to watch the same game. Have 'away' fans a more price inelastic demand as they are prepared to pay higher prices being a football club's most devoted supporters? The data below shows how the price charged on the M6 Toll varies according to vehicle type and the time of travel. It could be argued that only the price difference according to time of travel is an example of price discrimination. Heavy lorries impose much higher costs in road surface damage than cars and thus their toll should be higher.

M6 toll charges

Class	Mon-Fri (06:00-23:00)		Sat-Sun (06:00-23:00)		Night (23:00-06:00)	
	Non-Tag	Tag	Non-Tag	Tag	Non-Tag	Tag
Class 1 (e.g. motorbike)	£3.00	n/a	£2.80	n/a	£1.80	n/a
Class 2 (e.g. car)	£5.50	£5.23	£4.80	£4.56	£3.80	£3.61
Class 3 (e.g. car & trailer)	£10.00	£9.50	£8.60	£8.17	£6.60	£6.27
Class 4 (e.g. van or coach)	£11.00	£10.45	£9.60	£9.12	£8.60	£8.17
Class 5 (e.g. HGV or coach)	£11.00	£10.45	£9.60	£9.12	£8.60	£8.17

Source: M6 Toll (Midland Expressway Ltd)
Tag refers to a pre-payment system allowing regular uses to pass through the toll without stopping to pay cash.

A typical easyJet return flight from Luton to Malaga shown below shows major price differences depending upon when the booking was made.

Figure 8.8: Price discrimination

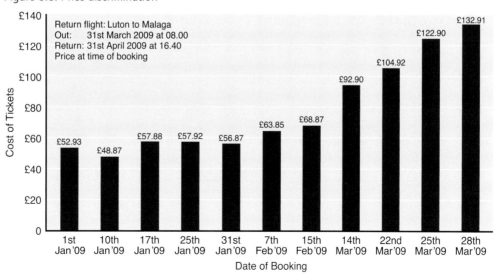

Price discrimination can spread demand away from peak-time use when travelling by train.

Airlines such as easyJet apply the principle of yield management when pricing their seats on flights, allowing them to maximise revenue from ticket sales.

Many producers deny that some of the examples above are price discrimination and argue that price differences reflect cost differences, a different service or exchange rate differences. It is often argued that price discrimination not only benefits producers with higher profits, but consumers who would not normally have bought the product if there were a single price may be tempted to buy at a special low off-peak price. Price discrimination also spreads demand away from peak-time use when travelling by train for example. Sometimes a firm will charge a higher price for its product in the home market where it faces little competition compared to the overseas market where the market is very competitive. There is no doubt that price discrimination by a profit maximising firm with some monopoly power will transfer some of the consumer surplus to the producer thus raising profit.

Is it worthwhile for a monopolist to advertise?

It would seem on the face of it that pure monopolists don't need to bother advertising as they have complete control of the market. However, advertising does help maintain the barriers to entry that exist against potential entrants, and it can be used to show that a monopolist is capable of being nice to consumers. In the past the water authorities in the UK, which are local monopolies, have often gone out of their way to inform their captive market that they are doing great things such as mending leaks and building new water treatment plants. In theory advertising will bring the monopolist even higher abnormal profits as the diagram below demonstrates. A successful advertising campaign will shift the demand curve to the right and assuming the cost structure remains the same abnormal profits will rise (Figure 8.9).

Figure 8.9: The increase in a monopolist's profit as a result of advertising

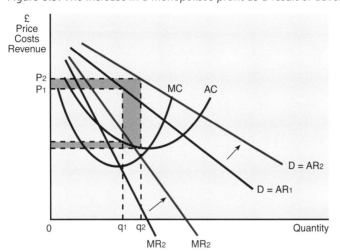

The benefits of monopoly	The drawbacks of monopoly
Abnormal profit provides funds for investment to maintain a competitive edge and also for R&D which are both important in global markets (dynamic efficiency).	Abnormal profit can mean little incentive to be efficient or to develop new products, leading to inefficiency.
There may be a need to match the large over-seas competitors in a global market. Monopolies may also be a powerful counterbalance to a powerful buyer (monopsony).	High prices and lower output for consumers. Reduced consumer surplus compared to a competitive market.
Cross-subsidisation of markets may lead to an increased range of goods or services available to the consumer. It can thus supply goods that would otherwise not be provided.	Monopolies can waste resources by cross-subsidisation, using profits from one part of their organisation to finance losses in another, which is useful when predatory pricing and limit pricing (these are anti-competitive practices). (See Unit 10)
Price discrimination may raise total revenue which allows the survival of a product or service. Price discrimination can benefit some consumers who pay a lower price.	Monopolies may engage in price discrimination to raise producer surplus and reduce consumer surplus. This may involve charging higher prices to consumers with inelastic demand.
Monopolies can take advantage of economies of scale which lowers cost per unit. If this lowers prices the consumer surplus is higher than competition.	Monopolies are allocatively and productively inefficient. They are also more likely to carry X-inefficiency. (See Unit 12)
Marginal cost pricing as practised in perfect competition does not cover fixed costs in declining cost industries leading to huge losses.	By setting a price above marginal cost, prices are above the resource cost of producing the product.
Monopolies avoid the problems of duplication and wasteful advertising and some industries are natural monopolies, e.g. local water companies? rail, gas and electricity infrastructures? (See Unit 12)	Monopolies deny consumers variety and choice which is available in competitive markets.

Source: Adapted from *Economics Made Simple*, G. Whitehead, with permission from Elsevier

The diagram below (Figure 8.10) can be used to show the disadvantages of monopoly. The price in a competitive market would be Pc where price = marginal cost. However a monopoly would charge Pm and quantity would fall to Qm. The effect is to reduce the consumer surplus and increase the producer surplus which obviously benefits the monopoly. The deadweight loss indicates the market failure resulting from the monopolisation of a competitive industry.

Figure 8.10

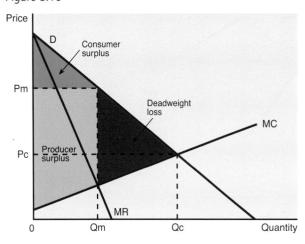

Question 8.1

A monopolist has separated its customers into two markets, A and B. The prices and quantities in these two markets are as follows:

Market A		Market B	
Price (£)	Quantity	Price (£)	Quantity
10	10	5.00	10
9	20	4.50	20
8	30	4.00	30
7	40	3.50	40
6	50	3.00	50
5	60	2.50	60
4	70	2.00	70
3	80	1.50	80
2	90	1.00	90
1	100	0.50	100

(a) What conditions are necessary for the monopolist to be able to separate the two markets in this case? *(2 marks)*

(b) (i) On graph paper plot the monopolist's demand and marginal revenue curves in markets A and B. *(4 marks)*

(ii) Assuming that the marginal cost of production is constant at £1.90, what quantity will the monopolist sell in each market if it is a profit maximiser? *(2 marks)*

(iii) What price will the monopolist charge in each market? *(2 marks)*

(c) Comment on the relationship between the price elasticity of demand and marginal revenue in market B. *(4 marks)*

(d) Assume that the monopolist now cuts its price in market A by £0.50. What is the price elasticity of demand at the new price charged? *(3 marks)*

(e) Assume that the monopolist now faces an increase in the business rates payable on its premises. How will the profit maximising monopolist adjust the prices charged in each market? *(3 marks)*

Source: ULEAC, Economics Paper 2, January 1989

Question 8.2

An economist can measure the monopoly power of a firm by using the following equation:

$$\frac{\text{Price} - \text{Marginal Cost}}{\text{Price}}$$

The closer the answer is to 1 the greater the degree of monopoly power exercised by the firm, and the closer it is to 0 the more competitive the market. Explain the reasoning behind this.

Question 8.3

The Economist newspaper is sold in newsagents for £4.00 but a recent special scheme allowed secondary school pupils to buy 30 copies for just £2.

(a) With the aid of a diagram explain why this is an example of second-degree price discrimination.

(b) Using the terms marginal cost and marginal revenue explain why *The Economist* may still make a profit from the papers it sells to schools at such a discount.

Question 8.4

Unlike many public corporations Royal Mail was not privatised in the 1980s or 1990s, and currently remains a state-owned company. However this has changed with the passing of the Postal Services Act 2011, which allows the government to privatise up to 90% of Royal Mail, with 10% being held by Royal Mail employees. Post Office Ltd will be separated from Royal Mail Group and will remain in public ownership. The Act also allowed for the assets and liabilities of the Royal Mail pension scheme to be taken over by the government. The privatisation process may be completed in 2014.

Royal Mail has seen postal volumes fall by 25% since 2006 as electronic and text messaging volumes have risen. They are expected to continue to fall 25-40% in the next five years. Last year Royal Mail's letters business, from which it gets more than two-thirds of its revenue, lost £120m. As a result Ofcomm, the regulator, recently allowed the price of stamps to rise to 50p (second class) and 60p (first class). Ofcom said that changes needed to be made to price limits because the future of the universal postal service – which guarantees a single price no matter where in the UK the letter is going – was at "severe risk".

The letters market has also been liberalised in recent years allowing private firms such as TNT and UK Mail to operate within the postal service. These firms bid for contracts to collect and sort bulk mail leaving the Royal Mail to deliver the letters through the letterboxes of firms and households (often called the last mile). Bulk mail contracts earn high revenues for these new entrants to the market; some call it cherry picking the most profitable activities. However, these firms have to pay the Royal Mail to complete the delivery and also the Royal Mail has an advantage in not being liable for VAT unlike their rivals.

Question: Is the collection, sorting and delivery of letters a natural monopoly?

Unit 9: **Monopolistic competition**

Few markets conform closely to the models of either perfect competition or monopoly. Between these two extremes lie two forms of imperfect competition, namely monopolistic competition and oligopoly.

Market characteristics

Monopolistic competition shares the characteristics of perfect competition, except for the fact that products are non-homogeneous (i.e. there is **product differentiation**). Product differentiation occurs either through real differences in products or differences in image for otherwise identical products (possibly created or reinforced by advertising).

Differences in products create scope for **brand loyalty**: A consumer might be willing to pay a higher price for the product of one firm than for that of another in the same market. Accordingly, the firm is not a price-taker, and each firm is faced by a downward sloping demand (AR) curve. Any firm raising its price will lose some business to its competitors, but brand loyalty will ensure that a firm will not suffer complete substitution away from its product. Because of the availability of substitutes the demand curve will be much more elastic than it would be for a monopolist operating in the same market. Good examples of monopolistic competition could include hairdressers and fast food outlets. High street chemists are an interesting example of a market, which is a partial example of monopolistic competition with the majority of the market in the hands of independent outlets. Independent chemists have about a 40% share of the UK market. There are also bigger firms in the market such as Boots and Tesco. The major supermarkets have also become increasingly involved in this sector, particularly since the ending of retail price maintenance on non-prescription drugs. Retail price maintenance meant that these products had to be sold at the same price in all retail outlets.

It is often confusing to students that a market structure with so little monopoly power for the firms is called monopolistic competition. The term 'monopolistic' refers to the small degree of monopoly power each firm possesses as a result of selling a branded product, which to some consumers will be unique.

They thus may see their local hairdresser, as the only place they would go to because they have been there for years and think the stylist is very good. The same can apply to restaurants. However, this monopoly power does not extend to all customers nor into the long run.

Short run equilibrium

The monopolistically competitive market conditions permit the possibility of short run supernormal profits (Figure 9.1) or losses.

Long run equilibrium

The lack of significant barriers to entry and exit ensures that normal profits are made in the long run. A situation of short run supernormal profit (as shown in Figure 9.1), for example, will induce new entry. As new firms enter the market, the demand curve facing any existing firm shifts to the left. It continues to do so until it is tangential to the average cost curve (AR = AC) at the profit maximising point. Given a situation of short run loss, some firms would leave the industry, restoring long run equilibrium.

Figure 9.1: Short run equilibrium under monopolistic competition

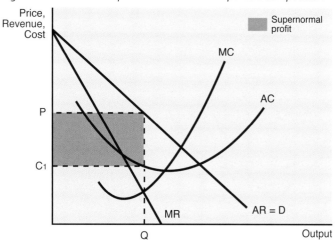

Figure 9.2 is a difficult one to draw. The following strategy is recommended:

1. Draw the average and marginal revenue curves.

2. Draw the average cost curve, with the point of tangency well above half way up the average revenue curve.

3. Label the price and quantity associated with this point of tangency (by virtue of the fact that the average revenue curve is also the demand curve).

4. Finally, draw the marginal cost curve. Ensure that it cuts the marginal revenue curve at the level of output depicted in step 3. It should also cut the average cost curve at that curve's lowest point.

Note that in the above diagram price is above marginal cost and output is below minimum efficient scale. This means that monopolistic competition is an allocatively and productively inefficient market (see Unit 12).

Figure 9.2: Long run equilibrium under monopolistic competition

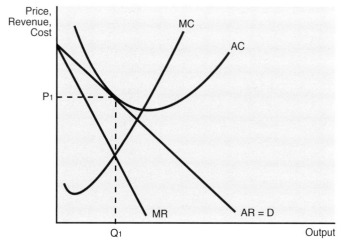

Question 9.1

Why might hairdressers, fast food outlets and Italian restaurants be examples of monopolistic competition?

Question 9.2

The diagram shows monopolistic competition in the short run with a firm making losses. Explain, using the diagram, how this firm's position would change in the long run if other loss-making firms left the industry.

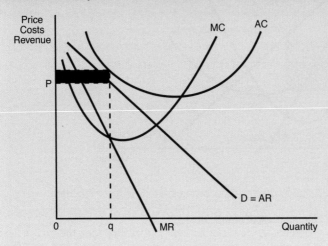

Question 9.3

Explain the main similarities and differences between perfect competition and monopolistic competition.

Unit 10: **Oligopoly**

Oligopoly occurs when a few firms between them share a large proportion of the output or sales. Oligopolistic markets have high levels of market concentration. Some oligopolies produce identical products (e.g. metals, sugar or cement) but most produce differentiated products (e.g. cars, soap powder and cigarettes). If the product is identical/homogeneous between firms then price competition or possibly a price fixing cartel is likely. With differentiated products non-price competition is likely with firms using advertising and brand proliferation as the main means of increasing market share at the expense of their competitors. A special case of oligopoly is **duopoly** which in its purest form means that only two producers exist in a market. In practice this definition can be relaxed when two firms dominate a market controlling a significant market share between them. There are two duopoly models Cournot and Bertrand. The Cournot model states that the two firms assume each other's output, treat this as a fixed amount and produce accordingly. In the Bertrand model each firm assumes that the other will not change prices in response to price cuts. When both firms use this logic in their strategies they will reach **Nash equilibrium**. Examples of duopoly in the real world include; Pepsi and Coca-Cola, aircraft manufacturers Airbus and Boeing and auctioneers Sotheby's and Christie's. However, duopolies can exist in market segments, for example until the recent takeover British Airways and BMI competed on the London Heathrow–Manchester route. Duopolies result in price and non-price competition and occasionally collusion. The salt which local councils spread on icy roads in the winter is supplied in the main by two firms in the UK, Salt Union (50%) and Cleveland Potash (35%), with the rest imported.

Market characteristics

1. A high market **concentration ratio** (the x-firm concentration ratio is the percentage of the market supplied by the largest x firms). Supply is concentrated in the hands of a few firms (see Unit 3). A better measure of market concentration is the **Herfindahl Index** which takes into account all the firms in an industry and their relative size distribution. The Herfindahl Index involves squaring the market shares of all the firms and then adding them together. A firm with a 20% market share would involve squaring 0.2. The final result will be between 0 and 1 and the nearer the result is to 1 the closer the market is to a monopoly. The index can also produce a result ranging up to 10,000 if the actual market share is used. Hence a duopoly with 50% each would give a Herfindahl Index of 2,500 + 2,500 = 5,000.

2. Firms are interdependent. With so few firms in the market, the actions of one firm will affect the other firms directly.

3. Barriers to entry and exit exist.

Because of the high degree of **interdependence**, oligopoly is a difficult market structure to analyse. The actions of a firm are determined not just by the actions of its rivals but also by the assumptions it makes about its rivals' possible reactions to its own initiatives.

Sweezy's theory of kinked demand

The assumptions of this theory help explain a tendency towards price rigidity often observed in oligopolistic markets. The theory assumes that any firm cutting its price is unlikely to enjoy much of a boost to demand as competitors will follow suit, while any firm raising its price will suffer a great loss of business as competitors are unlikely to follow. Thus the demand curve is kinked at the current price level, being elastic at higher prices and inelastic at lower prices. The firm then has no incentive to change price, and the vertical discontinuity produced in the MR curve by the kink in the AR curve offers another explanation of

price stability. The cost structure of the firm could change radically (MC1 → MC2) without a change in the profit maximising price.

Criticism's of Sweezy's theory include the lack of an explanation as to how the price reached its current level. The standard neo-classical short run profit maximising assumption, employed by Sweezy, is also questioned. However, a longer term view of profit maximisation (entailing a policy such as cost plus pricing) might also result in price stability (see Unit 5).

Figure 10.1: Sweezy's kinked demand curve

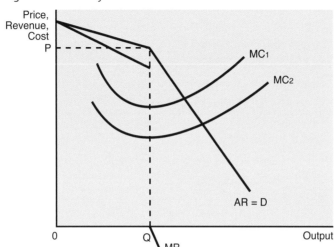

Game theory

In recent years game theory has become a popular way of examining the strategies that oligopolists may adopt in a market. When game theory is applied to oligopoly the players are firms, the game is played in the market, their strategies are their price/output decisions and the payoffs are their profits. Game theory involves studying the alternative strategies oligopolists may choose to adopt depending on their assumptions about their rivals' behaviour. Put at its simplest, if a firm is considering reducing its price, in making its decision it will need to take into account how its rival oligopolists might react and how it will affect them. Firms can choose high risk or low risk strategies in what is very similar to a game of poker between four or five players or chess between two players. The problem for firms is that they have imperfect knowledge of other firms' actions and reactions. Game theory was used by the UK government in 2000 when it raised £22.5bn from the telephone companies in an auction for the 3G mobile phone licences, which deliver voice, fax and video.

The auction took place in a sequence of rounds, with bids submitted by fax. In each round, participants bid simultaneously for any one of the five licences – with Licence A reserved for new entrants. At the end of each round, bidders were informed of all bids. The holder of the highest bid on each licence was required to remain inactive in following rounds until outbid. The auction ended when no more bids were received.

Thirteen firms started in the auction – the four existing mobile operators and nine potential new entrants. The top bidders after 126 rounds were Licence A, TIW, £4.1bn; Licence B, Vodafone, £5.1bn; Licence C, BT3G, £3.4bn; Licence D, One2One, £3.4bn; Licence E, Orange, £3.6bn. The four large existing operators, Vodafone, BT Cellnet, One2One and Orange led the bidding. Vodafone and BT's networks were overstretched and needed more capacity in order to get more customers, and thus they had to get one of the licences. The result was the phone companies paying much more than was expected for these licences which benefited the government and the tax payer.

Ofcom (the telecommunications and media regulator) has recently outlined plans for the 2012 auction of the valuable broadcast transmission spectrum that will be freed up by turning off the analogue television signal. The spectrum will be suitable for services such as ultra-fast wireless broadband and more digital terrestrial TV channels. Firms such as Dot Econ (http://www.dotecon.com) advise government and regulators such as Ofcom on how to conduct auctions of this kind. According to its web site: "Regulators now use auctions for divestments and DotEcon provides a one-stop shop for all aspects of designing and running auctions. Implementing an auction requires a wide range of skills particularly the use of **game theory** to understand how the auction design affects incentives."

In the table below firms X and Y are both selling their product in a duopolistic market for £1 and are separately thinking of cutting their prices to 80p. At £1 each firm makes a profit of £6m. Looking at firm X, if it left its price at £1 and Y cut its price to 80p then its profits would fall to £3.5m and Y's would rise to £7m. Alternatively if it cut its price to 80p and Y left its price at £1 then X's profits would rise to £7m. Both firms know that the other is thinking through the same strategies and so they both cut price to 80p and thus make £5m profit. This rational strategy poses the least risk and uncertainty for the two firms. If either left their price at £1, profits for either firm could fall to £3.5m. Clearly the option of collusion exists which gives them a chance of higher profits with price fixed at £1 by agreement or possibly **tacit collusion**.

Firm X's price

	£1	80p
£1	£6m each	£3.5m Y £7m X
80p	£7m Y £3.5m X	£5m each

Firm Y's price

Game theory suggests that firms don't trust each other and in the above matrix the two firms end up setting a price of 80p by attempting independently to choose their best strategy whatever the other firm's strategies could be. This is called the **Nash Equilibrium**.

The **prisoner's dilemma** is often used as an example to show how oligopolists have to face decisions on pricing. Two men are arrested for jointly committing a crime and are questioned separately. They know that if they both plead innocent they will be freed due to lack of evidence. Each is told by the police that if either one of them protests innocence while the other admits guilt the one who claims to be innocent will get a severe sentence while the other will be let off. If they both plead guilty, they will both get a less severe sentence. Both prisoners opt for a low risk strategy and plead guilty, as they are unable to communicate with one another. This is the outcome resulting from a low risk strategy by each prisoner, but if they had been allowed to co-operate they would have avoided prison all together. Oligopolists in the real world know that collusion is the profit-maximising outcome but there is then the concern that the competition authorities would investigate such behaviour. It can be argued that there is no need for formal collusion because, assuming perfect information and that each firm is rational, high prices are a natural outcome (see **tacit collusion**).

A **zero sum game** is one which whatever is won by one player/firm is lost by another. Such a strategy, which allows one firm to gain, must mean that another firm must lose. Some economists have argued that brand promotion by firms is a zero sum game. Special promotions and in-store displays can boost the sales of individual brands but overall total sales from all brands do not increase. The increased sales from the brands on promotion are taken from other brands that are not.

To compete or collude? Pricing strategy under oligopoly

If and when price stability under conditions of oligopoly breaks down, **price wars** frequently result (as illustrated by intense price competition with petrol retailing and air travel). The retail petrol market has

seen a number of such wars over the past two decades. It is in part because of the fear of price wars that oligopoly tends to be characterised by various forms of non-price competition.

It is often observed that oligopolistic firms are torn between two conflicting desires: the wish to compete on one hand, and the wish to collude on the other. The hope of winning any price war tempts some firms (particularly those with significant advantages, such as lower costs) but collusion is an attractive proposition given the desire to remove the uncomfortable uncertainty that interdependence brings to the market. Collusion reduces the fear of competitive price-cutting or retaliatory advertising, which could reduce industry profits.

(a) Collusion in oligopoly

Where oligopolists agree formally or informally to limit competition between themselves they may set output quotas, fix prices, or limit product promotion or development or even agree not to poach each other's markets.

A formal collusive agreement is called a **cartel**. A cartel can achieve the same profits as if the industry were a monopoly. In Figure 10.2 the total market or industry demand curve is shown as D and the corresponding marginal revenue curve is MR. The cartel's marginal cost curve (MC) is the horizontal sum of the marginal cost curves of the members of the cartel. The cartel will set a price of p1 (MC = MR) where profits are maximised. Alternatively the cartel could set output at q1 by giving each cartel member an output quota. This would produce the same price (p1).

By contrast, p2 shows the marginal cost price, which would be the price under perfect competition, with q2 showing the corresponding output. This means that the cartel will operate with a higher price and lower output when compared to perfect competition. The effect of the cartel is to reduce the consumer surplus and increase the producer surplus and **deadweight welfare loss** (shaded in the diagram).

Figure 10.2: Cartel with a monopoly price

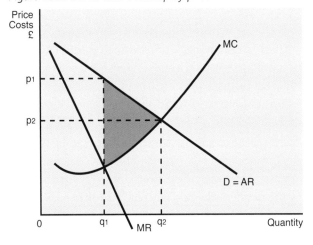

Covert collusion occurs where firms meet secretly and make decisions about prices or output. **Overt** collusive agreements are publicly made and are usually global in nature applying to particular commodities. OPEC, a group of petroleum exporting countries, sets production quotas for member countries to regulate the world price of oil. **Tacit collusion** is much more difficult to control. This is when firms act as if they have common pricing and output policies in place without actually having communicated with each other. The issue of tacit collusion is closely linked to **complex monopoly** theory.

Collusion between firms whether formal or informal is more likely when:

● there are only a few firms in the industry, so reaching an agreement is easier and any cheating can be spotted quickly.

● they have similar costs of production and methods of production making any agreement on price easier to reach.

● the firms produce homogeneous products where product differentiation is not a feature of the market. It is thus not surprising that cartels have been found in industries such as cement and heating oil in recent years. The EU competition authorities have dealt with EU-wide cartels in both glass and synthetic rubber in recent years.

● the products have price inelastic demand meaning that a rise in price by the cartel will lead to a rise in sales revenue for the firms.

● the laws against collusion in a country are weak or ineffective.

Collusive agreements often prove difficult to sustain. Most are illegal as they raise prices to the detriment of the consumer. They cannot, therefore, be enforced by contract, even if cheating could be detected. Each and every party to the collusive agreement has an incentive to cheat by producing more than agreed. This will suppress price slightly, but the firm can still take advantage of artificially high prices as long as the other firms do not cheat as well. However, stable market conditions (a small number of firms; similar costs of production; similar products; high barriers to entry; easy detection of cheating on the agreement) make joint profit maximisation feasible. The incentive to cheat among colluding firms can be assessed using game theory.

Cartels often have a limited life and there are many possible reasons for them breaking down. There is always a temptation for firms to increase their output above their quota to gain extra revenue – cheating by cartel members is common. In addition the entry of new firms into the market can undermine the cartel as non-cartel members sell their products at a price below those of cartel members. Increasing powers of regulators such as the Office of Fair Trading and the European Competition Commission have also made it difficult for cartel members to maintain agreements long term.

(i) Price leadership (dominant firm model)

One form of tacit collusion is where firms set the same price as an established price leader. The price leader is usually the 'dominant firm' in the market, this position being achieved through some factor such as size or cost advantage.

Figure 10.3 illustrates the dominant firm model. The dominant firm sets the price and then allows the other firms to supply as much as they wish at this price. The dominant firm supplies the remaining, or residual, market demand. This behaviour offers all firms the advantage of certainty; the dominant firm is able to set the price, while the remaining firms know that they will be able to supply as much as they wish at the price set.

Figure 10.3: The dominant firm model

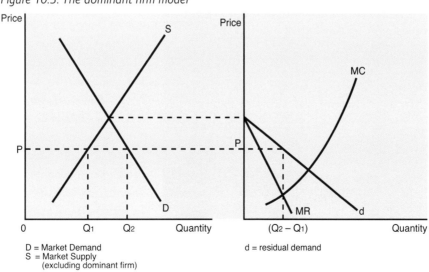

D = Market Demand
S = Market Supply
   (excluding dominant firm)

d = residual demand

Figure 10.4

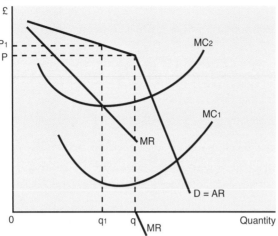

Another way of illustrating the dominant firm model is to return to the kinked demand curve as shown in Figure 10.4. The dominant firm is a low cost producer with marginal costs of MC1; a high cost rival firm would have higher marginal costs (MC2). The latter firm would like to charge a higher price than the dominant firm to maximise its profits but has to accept the profit maximising price set by the dominant firm who would not follow any price rise. The lower costs of the dominant firm would mean that a higher cost producer could not win a price war if it tried to cut the price set by the dominant firm at the kink.

Hence there is an identical price across the industry but this price favours the dominant firm.

(ii) Price leadership (barometric)

This occurs when a price change by one firm in an oligopoly as a result of changes in the macroeconomic environment (a recession) or market conditions in the industry (a rise in demand or input costs) results in all the other firms in the industry changing their prices by the same amount. Many analysts argued that

Has price leadership been operating in the UK energy market?

this has occurred in the UK energy sector in recent years when gas and electricity rose and fell by very similar amounts. If the firms have similar cost structures and maintain similar mark-ups this form of price leadership seems quite plausible especially if the product is homogeneous such as gas and electricity.

This is arguably shown in the table below with a price change by one firm being followed by the others. Bodies such as Consumer Focus have often felt that the UK energy **oligopoly** has been keen to pass on rising wholesale energy costs to customers in higher bills, but less enthusiastic to do so when they are falling. There have been many that have felt the energy market is rigged against consumers and the Labour Party Opposition in 2011 vowed to act against price-fixing by the six energy companies by requiring them to pool all energy centrally, a move that they claim would cut energy prices for 80% of users. Any company would then be able to buy and supply energy from the pool at a clear and transparent price.

Gas and electricity price changes 2010-2012

	Scottish Power	Scottish & Southern	British Gas	Npower	E.On	EDF
Nov 2010	🔥 2% ⚡ 8.9%					
Dec		🔥 9.4%	🔥 7% ⚡ 7%			
Jan 2011				🔥 5.1% ⚡ 5.1%		
Feb					🔥 3% ⚡ 9%	
Mar						🔥 6.5% ⚡ 7.5%
Aug	🔥 19% ⚡ 10%		🔥 18% ⚡ 16%			
Sept		🔥 18% ⚡ 11%			🔥 18% ⚡ 11%	
Oct				🔥 15.7% ⚡ 7.2%		
Nov						🔥 15.4% ⚡ 4.5%
Jan 2012			⚡ -5%			
Feb				🔥 -5%		🔥 -5%
Mar		🔥 -4.5%				

Source: Major energy suppliers and news websites   🔥 = Gas ⚡ = Electricity

Many feel that **tacit collusion** is present in this market although customers themselves have often failed to make the effort to take advantage of cheaper energy deals by investigating different suppliers. This is called **customer inertia**. However, at the same time many household and business energy users have been confused by the complex pricing structure used by the energy companies – there are 300 different tariffs! The regulator Ofgem has said in 2011 that the whole market needs to be simplified and suppliers must provide one, comparable, unit rate price giving greater transparency for consumers. However, despite suspicions of collusion the companies have not, as yet, been referred to the **Competition Commission**.

(iii) Complex monopolies

A complex monopoly is said to exist when a market is served by at least two firms which are not interconnected who engage in conduct, whether by collusion or not, which is likely to restrict, distort or prevent competition. The firms in question would have to control at least 25% of the market for the public interest to be damaged though. The firms, although pursuing individual non-collusive policies, behave in a uniform manner resulting in a situation, which appears as though they have colluded. In recent years the UK Competition Commission has found that the major supermarkets and the big commercial banks belong to complex monopolies. Hanson Cement, owned by HeidelbergCement, meets 25% of the demand for cement in the UK- a product which is homogeneous to a large extent. With just a few major producers this is a market where a complex monopoly may act against the consumers' interests, in this case the building and construction industry.

Can collusion ever be in the public interest?

In theory a price fixing cartel will reduce the consumer surplus, increase the producer surplus and bring

about a welfare loss. However, it has been argued that in certain circumstances a cartel produces industry wide benefits that are arguably in the public interest. For example many have applauded the collective selling of television rights for coverage of sport. In 2005 the European Union (EU) Competition Commission initially felt that the FA Premier League of 20 clubs was against the public interest as it is a cartel. However, it can be argued that such collective selling protects the smaller clubs in the Premier League and brings more money into football than if the clubs each negotiated their own television deals in an open competitive market. The same principle has been argued in relation to Britain's 60 racecourses that have collectively sold their television rights. Racing UK is a subscription-only television channel which broadcasts horse racing from 30 UK courses. These courses are effectively the owners of the channel which was launched in 2004 – after racecourses were given the freedom to collectively negotiate their own broadcasting rights. The other 30 UK race courses (including seven owned by Arena Leisure) broadcast their races on At The Races channel. Recent television deals negotiated between the FA Premier League and television broadcasters include a Competition Commission stipulation that the League cannot sell all their television rights to one buyer, which in the past has been BskyB. From the start of the 2013-14 season 154 matches will be shown live, five packages of 26 matches and two packages of 12. However one single broadcaster will be limited to owning four of the 26 match packages plus one of the 12 match packages. Some would argue that selling television rights in sport is a special case and normal rules of free competition are not in the public interest.

A cartel tends to protect its weakest members which might exit the market if there was competition. However, in sport, particularly football, a cartel by collectively negotiating television rights prevents the larger clubs being so dominant that the league becomes uncompetitive. For example in the English Premier League games involving top clubs such as Manchester United v Arsenal would earn very high television revenues whereas a game such as Stoke City v Norwich City would not.

It is important to distinguish collusion from co-operation by firms or **joint ventures**. The strategic airline alliances such as 'One World' and 'Star Alliance' arguably benefit the long haul traveller as well as the airlines by producing lower costs. Airbus is a joint venture of European aircraft manufacturers and without the competition from Airbus, Boeing would enjoy a virtual monopoly. Motor manufacturers have often co-operated in the high cost and high risk areas of product development, e.g. fuel cell technology. The Eurofighter is also a co-operative venture of several firms.

(b) Competitive pricing

(i) Entry limit pricing (limit pricing)
This policy entails charging the highest price compatible with deterring new entry to the market. The price is set below the profit maximising level, because of the fear that this price will be sufficiently high to attract new firms into the market. Limit pricing is discussed in more detail in Unit 11.

(ii) Predatory pricing
A predatory pricing policy is designed to force competitors out of the market. If a firm believes that it can sustain a very low price for longer than its rivals, it might charge such a price on a temporary basis. Usually the predator will set a price below average variable cost. When the target of the policy has been forced out of business, the predator will then raise its price to the profit maximising level. Such policies constitute an anti-competitive practice and are therefore outlawed by UK competition law (see Unit 15).

In the past large bus companies in the UK have been accused of predatory pricing. They allegedly used the profits made from high fares on routes where they faced no competition to subsidise very low fares on routes where they faced competition from small operators. By setting fares below average variable costs the larger operators could drive the new entrants out of the market. When Stelios Haji-Ioannou launched easyBus in 2004 he accused National Express, a well established operator, of predatory pricing on his Milton Keynes to London route.

In 2005 Tesco was accused of predatory pricing by the Association of Convenience Stores. Increasingly Tesco and Sainsbury are opening small grocery outlets to serve a local community (Tesco Express). Independent grocery stores have traditionally served this market. In 2005 a small Tesco opened in Withernsea, an East Yorkshire town, and sent 6,000 households £8 discount vouchers if £20 was spent in the local Tesco store. This was the equivalent of a 40% discount. It has been alleged that this was predatory pricing designed to force small grocers out of the market. In recent years small independently owned petrol stations have objected to planning application by supermarkets such as Tesco claiming that they often use a "predatory" pricing policy of selling fuel below cost to get people into the supermarket to buy groceries but often raising the price once the local petrol retail competition had been eliminated. However such activities have to be sustained for a period of time before the Office of Fair Trading can take action against a predator under the terms of the Competition Act.

(iii) Marginal cost pricing

This pricing policy is most likely in industries in public ownership or in industries in private hands, which are being regulated by a government agency.

Such pricing maximises consumer welfare and leads to an optimum allocation of resources. Consumers pay a price, the valuation they place upon the product, that is equal to the cost of producing one extra unit of output, the resource cost (i.e. price = marginal cost which is allocatively efficient).

Figure 10.5(i): Marginal cost pricing

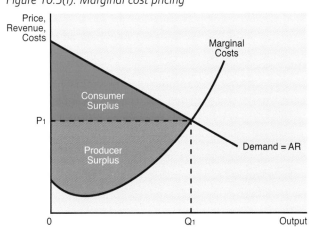

At price OP1 in Figure 10.5(i), the industry is to supply output OQ1 and the community surplus is maximised. (The benefits obtained by both consumers and producers – but not paid for.) This is said to be the output level that maximises social benefit. If marginal cost pricing is abandoned as in Figure 10.5(ii) and the price reverts to a profit maximising price, the shaded area represents the **deadweight welfare loss** of such a price change.

Figure 10.5(ii)

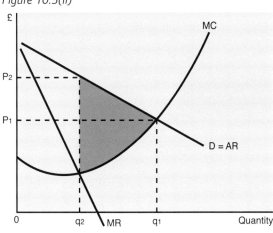

Practical difficulties in marginal cost pricing

1. MC pricing fails to take into account changes in demand, particularly for gas, electricity, transport and telecommunications, where demand varies daily, weekly and from season to season.

   For example, commuter trains are crowded during the 'rush hour' but have few passengers for the rest of the day; at peak periods, to carry one extra passenger may require an extra train service, whilst, at off-peak periods, the marginal cost of carrying an extra passenger is virtually zero. Such variations in demand make it very hard to estimate marginal cost realistically.

2. In integrated systems of production, such as the electricity industry, marginal cost is very hard to identify. For example, an increase in the price of oil which raises the MC of generating electricity in oil-fired power stations by say 10% does not enable the industry to increase price by exactly 10%. This is because a single consumer, through the grid system, might be consuming electricity generated in nuclear or coal-fired power stations where marginal costs are unchanged. The problem facing the industry is to estimate the overall increase in the marginal cost of the system. '**Unbundling**' the costs in such a complex market is thus very difficult, and poses a problem for regulators.

   To understand 'unbundling' think of a food hamper you may receive from a department store. If you want to unbundle the cost of the hamper you need to find the price of each item of food in the hamper by visiting the store. In an industry the unbundling of costs is the process of identifying each distinct aspect of the provision of a product or service and determining its cost. It can be used in the regulation of privatised utilities such as electricity supply which is sub-divided into generation, transmission, and distribution. In telephone services where BT own the network but there are other providers to consumers who need to access this network unbundling costs are also an issue.

3. Marginal cost pricing may cause an industry with decreasing long-run costs (a national monopoly perhaps) to encounter financial deficits (see Figure 10.6). The loss arises because the enterprise charges a price below long-run average cost and so is unable to generate sufficient revenue to replace worn out equipment and plant. This applies particularly to businesses such as railways which have decreasing long-run costs with an extensive track, signaling, and stations network. If marginal cost pricing were applied to household consumers of water who were using a metering system, then a standing fixed charge would have to be applied to cover the high fixed costs of pipeline and drainage systems that are needed in water infrastructure. In these declining cost industries marginal cost pricing does not cover the full cost of provision. Figure 10.7 does show that marginal cost pricing can give a firm abnormal profits in some circumstances.

Figure 10.6: Losses with marginal cost pricing

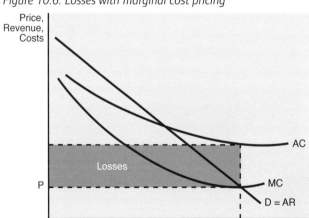

4. The marginal cost-pricing rule is designed to achieve **Pareto efficiency** in the allocation of resources (see page 69). But, when there are externalities, this should be incorporated into the estimates of marginal costs and benefits.

5. If marginal costs are rising sharply and demand is high the firm will make abnormal profits, as can be seen in Figure 10.7.

Figure 10.7: Abnormal profits with marginal cost pricing

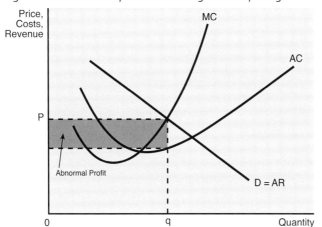

Non-price competition

This can take a variety of forms including product differentiation, product development and sales promotion. The policies have three broad aims: expanding the total market; expanding the individual firm's share of the existing market; and fostering brand loyalty which will make the firm's demand less price elastic. A successful advertising campaign will shift the demand curve to the right and decrease elasticity. Consumers' brand loyalty will thus make them less sensitive to price changes. In recent years retailers, especially supermarkets, to build brand loyalty, have used loyalty cards such as Nectar extensively. Buyers of petrol will go to BP regularly to collect Nectar points when petrol may be cheaper elsewhere. Newspapers have also used free DVDs, CDs and posters to entice people to buy a copy of their latest edition. Such non-price competition tends to reduce the risk of price competition, which can sometimes lead to a damaging price war.

Question 10.1

Show diagrammatically the effect of the accomplishment of each of the aims of non-price competition on the demand curve for a firm's product.

Question 10.2

Using the links below investigate the cartels featured and how they were dealt with by the competition authorities.

http://www.bbc.co.uk/news/business-14483959

http://www.bbc.co.uk/news/business-13064928

http://www.bbc.co.uk/news/business-11719507

Unit 11: **Contestable markets theory**

Amongst the chief determinants of a firm's behaviour, according to neo-classical theory, is the number and size of its competitors. The key insight offered by its relatively new 'rival', the contestable markets approach is that *potential* competitors (not yet in existence, or at least not operating in this market) can have an important influence on the conduct of the firm. The theory came to prominence in the early 1980s, largely through the work of William Baumol.

Clearly in many markets the mere **threat of entry** by new firms will affect the behaviour of incumbent firms. If there is the possibility of a new firm coming into the market the incumbent firms may respond by cutting costs to become more competitive or they may engage in limit pricing. If the potential entrant is very small, maybe aiming for a niche market and posing no real threat to the established firms the latter may not have any need to change their behaviour. In some markets existing firms may always behave as if there is a threat of entry whether a threat currently exists or not.

The degree of contestability of a market is measured by the extent to which the gains from market entry for a firm exceeds the cost of entering (i.e. the cost of overcoming barriers to entry), with the risks associated with failure taken into account (the cost associated with any barriers to exit). Accordingly, the levels of **barriers to entry and exit** are crucial in determining the level of a market's contestability. Barriers to exit consist of **sunk costs**, that is to say costs that cannot be recovered when leaving the market. The contestable markets approach suggests that potential entrants consider post-entry profit levels, rather than the pre-entry levels suggested by neo-classical theory.

In theory perfect competition is a perfectly contestable market and in between that and blockaded entry are varying degrees of contestability. Monopolistic competition has minimal entry barriers although small firms need to build up a customer base and meet certain government regulations. Oligopolies tend to be much less contestable with high capital expenditure and advertising costs to name but two entry barriers. **Blockaded entry** arises when a firm is protected by a legal monopoly, which the Post Office still has to a diminishing extent with the letterpost delivery. It can also occur when a firm has the protection of a patent, which gives the producer the intellectual property rights to be a legal monopolist for a limited time period.

Obviously no market is perfectly contestable, i.e. with zero sunk costs. In modern economies it is the degree of contestability, which is relevant, some markets are more contestable than others. Also just because there have been no new entrants to a market over a given period of time does not mean that this market is not contestable. The threat of entry will be enough to make the existing (incumbent) firms behave in such a way as to recognise this, i.e. by setting a price which doesn't attract entry and which only makes normal profits.

In Figure 11.1 a monopolist is making abnormal profits (shown by the coloured area) in a perfectly contestable market. If there are no entry or exit barriers new firms will enter the market attracted by the high profits. The monopolist is then forced to reduce price to P2 where sales volume is maximised and normal profits are earned (AC = AR), when trying to assess the contestability of a market. Technological change can make a market more contestable e.g. the Internet has allowed new firms into many markets. Some markets are less contestable because of the high level of expenditure on such things as infrastructure e.g. water pipelines, where very strong brands exist in a market, or where new entrants will have to spend heavily on advertising. Witness the ultimately futile attempt by ITV Digital in 2001 to break into the market for pay TV where Sky was an established brand. The failure of ITV (a huge established broadcaster) is in stark contrast to the initial success of Setanta Sports which was formed only in 1990 as an outlet for Irish sporting events to Irish expatriates. This firm made a successful entry into subscription sports broadcasting helped partly by a European Commission ruling which prevented BSkyB buying the rights to all of the English Premier League's games. However, in 2009 Setanta UK went into administration as the number of subscribers failed to reach the break-even point for survival. Setanta Sports continues to operate successfully in Ireland, Canada and Australia. In addition established firms know far more about an industry and how it works than potential entrants. Well established firms have well developed data bases relating to their customers and suppliers which new entrants will have to build up over time. This information imbalance works against potential entrants who will realise that it takes time to acquire this knowledge. Markets will also be less contestable if the established firms have a reputation for limit pricing, putting off new entrants. This issue is dealt with in the next section.

Figure 11.1: Contestable markets

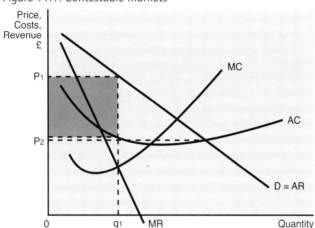

Entry limit pricing (limit pricing)

The fear on the part of existing firms of rendering the market contestable (stimulating new entry) by making high levels of profit is likely to lead to the adoption of entry limit pricing, a concept introduced in the previous unit. This is essentially a defensive strategy, with existing firms setting prices as high as possible but not so high as to enable new-comers to enter the industry. Limit pricing works effectively when the established firms have lower costs than the potential entrant. In the diagram below (Figure 11.2) the long run average costs of the established firms are represented by $LRAC_1$ and the potential entrant's by $LRAC_2$. When there is no threat of entry the established firm sets its price at a profit maximising P_1, but if there is a threat of entry the established firm sets a limit price of P_L which is equal to the long run average cost of the potential entrant. Entry by a new firm would add extra production to the industry increasing output beyond q_L to say q_2. This extra output will depress price to P_2 and make entry by the potential entrant unprofitable as the market price would now be below its long run average cost ($LRAC_2$).

Figure 11.2: Entry limit pricing

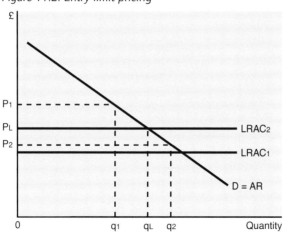

A market with no barriers to entry or exit would be considered perfectly contestable. Entry limit pricing in such a market would entail setting price equal to average cost, so that only normal profits are made. Where barriers to entry and exit exist limit pricing provides scope for supernormal profits to be made; the higher the barriers the higher the profits that can be made by deterring entry. In summary, contestable markets theory predicts that firms might be forced to set price as though operating in a competitive market even in the absence of actual competition. The lower the barriers to entry and exit, the greater the extent to which prices will be set at this level.

If existing firms choose not to adopt entry limit pricing, the potential exists for contestable markets to be highly unstable. Markets, which are highly contestable, are likely to be vulnerable to '**hit and run competition**'. Consider a situation where existing firms are pricing at above the entry-limit level. Even in the event that existing firms react in a predatory style, new entry will be profitable as long as there is a time lag between entry and the implementation of such action. Having made a profit in the intervening period, the new entrant can then leave the market at very little cost. The double-glazing industry is one area that exhibits behaviour compatible with this theory. The market in many regions is dominated by a number of firms that have had a long-term presence in the industry, but who are frequently challenged by new entrants, many of whom leave the market after a short time.

The order in which firms enter a particular market can have a significant effect on the conduct of firms and the behaviour of customers. The first significant firm to enter a new market is called the first mover. This firm has advantages from this and there are several **first mover advantages**. These include the opportunity for this firm to establish a good reputation and gain brand loyalty possibly making demand for their product price inelastic. Secondly customers who initially buy the first mover's product may find it difficult to switch to the products of subsequent entrants. This is best illustrated with the Apple i-Pod (a first mover), because any songs downloaded via Apple's i-Tunes were not able to be transferred to other MP3 players.

Clearly first movers may face disadvantages though. Specifically, later entrants can sometimes copy the technology used by first movers, although the latter will probably have gained some patent protection for this. Late entrants are also able to take advantage of the mistakes made by first movers who are often on a steep learning curve when operating in a new market. These firms may be able to adapt to changing technological and market conditions more effectively than the first mover.

Question 11.1

What factors may have led to both the banking and airline industries becoming more contestable in recent years?

Unit 12: **Economic efficiency and the conditions necessary for its attainment**

Economic efficiency is concerned with the relationship between production and the scarce inputs used. In other words, how well are resources combined to produce an end result?

1. **Productive efficiency.** This entails operating at the lowest possible average cost of production, and attainment is therefore dependent on reaping all available economies of scale (long run cost savings derived from the size of the firm). See point A on Figure 12.1.

2. **Technical efficiency.** This is achieved when any given output is produced with the minimum quantity of inputs. By implication, any point on the long-run average cost curve, which represents the minimum level of cost for any given output, is technically efficient. Production above the curve is not, the inefficiency involved sometimes being known as **x-inefficiency** (see point B below).

Figure 12.1: Technical and productive efficiency

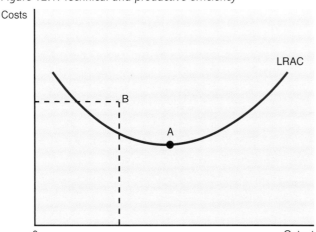

3. **Allocative efficiency.** This deals with the issue of whether resources are allocated to producing the goods and services that people want. In other words, does the allocation of resources maximise society's utility (benefit)? It would, of course, be possible for us to make goods using productively efficient processes yet for no one to want the end product. There was never enough demand for ITV Digital, for example, and to devote large quantities of resources to its production was inefficient. As a result its parent TV companies, Granada and Carlton, closed it down in 2002.

The charge of allocative inefficiency was often levelled at centrally planned (command) economies (such as the Soviet Union), because it is difficult for planners to gauge the public's wishes accurately. An advantage of the market economy is that because firms make profits by satisfying the demands of the consumer, the consumer is sovereign and dictates which goods and services are produced.

Figure 12.2 depicts the supply curve, drawn on the assumption of a perfectly competitive market, and equal to the marginal cost (MC) of production. The demand curve informs us of the price associated with any given level of demand. This price will equal the marginal private benefit (MPB) or satisfaction derived from the last unit of consumption, as we can expect consumers to demand an extra unit of a product as long as MPB exceeds the cost of consumption (i.e. the price, P): It is only when MPB has declined to the point where it equals price that no further units will be demanded. Any level of output to the left of Q (the competitive equilibrium output) does not maximise utility net of costs, since here an extra unit of output will add more to utility than costs. To the right of Q, MC exceeds MPB, suggesting

Figure 12.2: Allocative efficiency

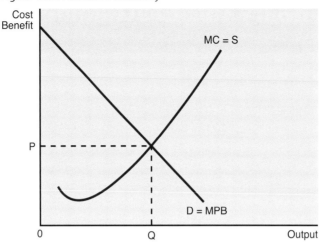

that the last unit produced caused a loss of utility net of costs. Consequently, Q must maximise society's net benefit and must be the allocatively efficient output level. Here, MPB is equated to MC; since MPB is in turn equal to price, allocative efficiency is achieved where:

$$P = MC$$

Given that output level Q is the competitive equilibrium level of output, we can conclude that perfectly competitive markets are allocatively efficient.

It should be noted that the P = MC condition does not secure the attainment of allocative efficiency where externalities (costs or benefits that accrue to third parties as a result of the activities of other economic agents) are present. The analysis above assumes the private costs and benefits to be the only costs and benefits to society (see Unit 16 on market failure).

4. **Distributive efficiency.** The goods produced should be distributed precisely to those consumers desiring them.

5. **Dynamic efficiency.** This is concerned with the efficient allocation of resources over time. Dynamic efficiency is concerned with innovation and investment which will reduce the long run average cost curve. Invention in new machines, new technology and more efficient working practices will shift the long run average cost curve from LRAC1 to LRAC2 (Figure 12.3). Obviously improving dynamic efficiency does involve an increase in costs in the short term but the benefits will be seen in the long run. Its attainment is likely to entail investing a substantial quantity of the resources available today, either to improve the capital stock or to further research and development.

Figure 12.3

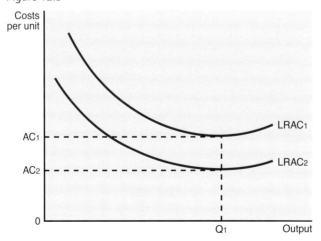

Dynamic efficiency is concerned with innovation and investment which will reduce the long run average cost curve.

In order to establish objective criteria for efficiency, economists often use '**Pareto Efficiency**'. A Pareto efficient allocation of resources is said to exist if it is not possible to reallocate resources so as to improve the well being (or utility) of one person without making at least one person worse off (reduce their utility). The Pareto criterion enables us to assess efficiency but does not say anything about equity. For any economy, there are a number of efficient allocations, some of which will involve more equity in distribution between individuals in the society than others. The Pareto criterion cannot distinguish between these.

Figure 12.4: Pareto efficiency

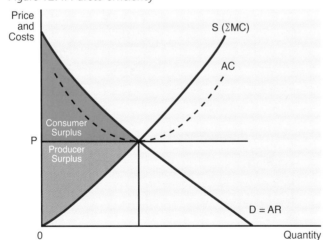

The conditions for Pareto efficiency will exist when there is perfect competition in all markets. If there were perfect competition in all markets, it is theoretically possible for an allocation of resources to be achieved which is optimal (or efficient) for society as a whole. At the simplest level, we can see that a competitive firm will produce at the lowest point on its average cost curve (productive efficiency). In addition if price = marginal cost (MC) consumers are paying a price exactly equal to the **marginal utility** (MU) or extra satisfaction they receive from the last unit consumed (P = MU) and producers are receiving exactly the

marginal cost of producing that unit (P = MC) (allocative efficiency). The combined consumer surplus and producer surplus (the community surplus) are both maximised (see Figure 12.4).

Thus in an efficient economy when price equals marginal cost in all industries no consumer who values a commodity more than it costs society to produce it will be deterred from buying it. However, the **theory of second best** states that if price is higher than marginal cost in one industry it is not efficient for the price to equal marginal cost in all other industries. This would just encourage over consumption of the cheaper goods priced at marginal cost. Many years ago in the 1960's when the UK had a sizeable proportion of economic activity in the hands of state-owned (nationalised) firms the government directed a marginal cost pricing policy to the managements of these firms. However, with so many private sector firms pricing their products above marginal cost this can result in over consumption and production in the nationalised sector. In addition in such industries with high fixed costs, rail and electricity generation for example, marginal cost pricing just led to enormous losses being made because the fixed costs were never covered.

Comparing market structures from an efficiency and performance perspective

We begin by comparing the efficiency of monopoly and perfect competition in two ways:

1. A comparison of a competitive firm with its monopolistic counterpart (Figure 12.5) reveals that the competitive firm achieves both productive and allocative efficiency while the monopolist achieves neither:

2. A more sophisticated approach is to compare the competitive industry's outcomes with those of the *same* industry under monopoly (Figure 12.6).

Figure 12.5: A simple comparison of monopoly and perfect competition

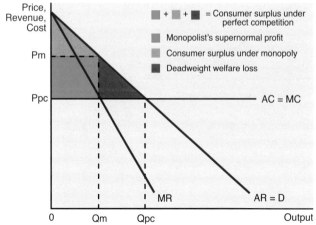

Figure 12.6: A more sophisticated comparison of monopoly and perfect competition

Recall that under perfect competition, all firms produce at the lowest possible average cost and all firms have identical cost curves. We assume now that a monopolist buys up all the firms. Each would be run as a separate plant, with no attempt made to merge plants, because this would result in increased average costs. If the monopolist wished to expand output, it would do so by opening another plant of the same size, producing at the same AC. Accordingly, the monopolist's long run average cost curve is horizontal, equal to constant marginal costs.

If the industry were competitive, it would produce at the point on the demand curve where P (= MPB) = MC (output Qpc). However, the monopolist will maximise profits by equating MR and MC (at output Qm), and allocative inefficiency results (Pm > MC). The monopolist is thus accused of exploiting the consumer by restricting output and raising price. The allocative inefficiency results in a **deadweight welfare loss** as shown. In defence of monopoly, we can raise Schumpeter's argument that monopoly profits provide funds for research and development (dynamic efficiency).

The case of **natural monopoly** is relevant here. There are some industries (typically those requiring huge expenditure on infrastructure, such as the rail industry) where economies of scale are so large that competition would be neither efficient nor profitable. Electricity and gas infrastructures (wires and pipes) are good examples of natural monopolies and in the UK are owned by one company (National Grid). Competing energy suppliers to households and firms pay National Grid to access the network; this arrangement is called common carriage and could be extended to water supply which at present is a regional monopoly. Figure 12.7 shows economies of scale so large that not even a single producer could fully exploit them. Splitting the profit maximising output (Q) in two (Q/2) would raise average costs substantially (AC1 to AC2). Allocatively efficient production (P = MC) would result in a loss. The problem being that some natural monopolies have continuously falling average costs. Thus MC cuts the demand curve below the AC curve.

Figure 12.7: Natural monopoly

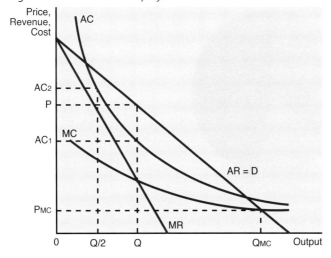

Question 12.1

Social efficiency occurs when social welfare is maximised by a firm in a market. This occurs at the level of output where the marginal social benefit equals the marginal social cost. This means that the firm takes into account external costs and benefits as well as its internal or private costs and benefits.

Draw a diagram showing a firm producing at its socially efficient level of output and how it differs from the free market level of output.

Unit 13: **Monopsony**

Monopsony arises in a market when there is a single buyer of a product or factor of production (usually labour). Oligopsony arises when there are a few large buyers in a market. In product markets there has been concern in the UK in recent years that large retail chains such as Tesco, Asda and Sainsbury have such a large degree of buying power over suppliers such as food producers and farmers that they are able to force down the prices paid to them. This buying power goes beyond discounts being offered for bulk purchases, which is associated with **economies of scale**. Rather this has allegedly taken the form of the buyer stating the price to the supplier on a take it or leave it basis. Prices paid to suppliers such as farmers have allegedly been changed at will by the supermarkets as no formal contracts were even drawn up between the buyer and the supplier.

Concern over excessive buyer power has been one of the factors that has prompted the Competition Commission investigation into the UK supermarket sector on more than one occasion in the last few years. Competition Commission analysis has covered both the supermarkets' relationships with suppliers and the extent to which the downstream market was competitive. The investigation of the latter included an analysis of price trends over time, international price comparisons, and profitability and consumer satisfaction. The Competition Commission concluded that there was no evidence of excess prices or profits and that the market was 'broadly competitive'. There is always the issue of the possible existence of a **complex monopoly** and **tacit collusion** in the UK supermarket sector (Figure 13.1).

Figure 13.1: Market share of supermarkets

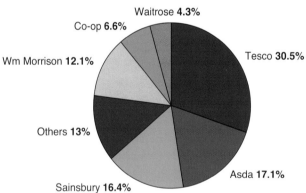

The Competition Commission's analysis of supplier relations was equally comprehensive. One of the chief complaints against the supermarkets has been that lower wholesale prices in certain product categories (particularly meat products) has not been passed on to consumers and this was cited as evidence of the adverse impact on consumers of the large retailers' buyer power. For meat products, the Competition Commission found that cost reductions at the supplier level had been passed through to retail prices or, where they had not, that there had been cost increases elsewhere in the supply chain. In other areas, however, the Competition Commission was critical of the large supermarkets in their dealings with suppliers. It identified a number of practices (such as requiring suppliers to pay for better product positioning within stores), which it believed could be detrimental to competition in supplier markets. The Competition Commission recommended that a **Code of Practice** be drawn up to address its concerns, which was introduced in 2002. In 2001 small dairy farmers complained that the fall in the price of milk paid to them by the large dairies was not reflected in supermarket milk prices. Prices are below variable costs of production forcing farmers to leave the dairy sector. Dairy farmers are thus possibly the victims of the excessive buying power of the dairies and supermarkets. Individually they are too small to be anything but

price takers and victims of buyer-power. In 1995 the supermarkets kept 3% of the retail price of a pint of milk but by 2007 it was over 31%.

Many farmers are not brave enough to speak publicly about supermarket practices which keep prices to suppliers down. Farmers and suppliers allege that they operate in a climate of fear not daring to complain for fear of losing the supermarkets' custom. Farmers who have left the business complain that the amount they were 'paid' by supermarkets was often reduced by up to a half because they had to pay for packaging, labelling and distribution to another company. Some allege that if a supermarket runs a 'buy one get one free' offer then it is the supplier that has to pay for it. For many suppliers the lack of a contract stating how much they would be paid has been a major issue. Many say that they had to pay up front to be a preferred supplier- buying the right to supply a supermarket.

The controversy over the relationship between the supermarkets and their suppliers led to the **Competition Commission** in 2008 calling on the Department for Business, Innovation and Skills (BIS) to install an ombudsman who would be responsible for investigating complaints levelled at grocery retailers under a revised Grocery Supply Code of Practice which became effective in early 2011. The move followed an inquiry into grocery supplies and several failed attempts to encourage retailers, particularly the large supermarkets, to co-operate with an earlier voluntary code of practice to safeguard the interests of suppliers.

The work of the Ombudsman or Groceries Code Adjudicator (GCA) was not expected to start until the summer of 2013 because of delays in the legislative process. The delay had dismayed suppliers' groups such as the National Farmers Union (NFU). It was concerned that, while the Government introduced a Groceries Supply Code of Practice (GSCOP) in February 2011, there had been no one to police it since then. The NFU say that dairy producers have been particularly hit by the buying power of supermarkets. Shoppers can pay about £1.70 for two litres of milk for which the farmer receives less than 50p. There is also disquiet among suppliers that the GCA will not initially fine supermarkets that breached the new code of practice, which applies to the 10 companies with turnover in excess of £1bn. Instead, ministers will "name and shame" those grocers that breach the rules, believing that lost sales and a damaged reputation among the public is a bigger penalty for supermarkets to pay.

It is alleged that supermarkets have been stating their prices to suppliers on a take it or leave it basis.

The problem of monopsony power has also arisen in the care home market for the elderly as a result of the buying power of the social services departments of the English local authorities. Local authorities finance nursing home care to those who cannot afford it and as a result block purchase a significant amount of the capacity in the care home sector on behalf of their patients. This buying power has allegedly allowed them to drive down the fees that the care homes can charge to such a low level that many cannot make a profit. Some of these homes charge higher fees to other patients who have the means to pay and who don't use social services. This pricing policy allows the homes to survive but is a form of **price discrimination** that is arguably an unfair outcome from the abuse of monopsony power. An interesting result of this situation has been the emergence of large nursing home groups such as Care UK and Four Seasons who own several care homes. The tendency for powerful sellers to emerge to balance the strength of powerful buyers such as the local authorities is an example of **countervailing power**.

Even the large care home groups have been finding the going tough, as evidenced by the collapse of Southern Cross in 2011. Local authorities and the government are the purchasers of 63% of care home places and at the moment they are not paying the true cost of care which puts enormous strain on the care home sector. As the care home sector is privately owned the businesses are profit motivated and thus the present system is arguably unsustainable.

The problem is inflamed by the local authorities having insufficient funding to pay a true market price for the care home beds they purchase. They may be acting like a monopsonist but it is through necessity rather than greed.

In 2005 the retailer Halfords was accused by its suppliers of abusing its dominant buying position. The car parts group (which is twelve times bigger than its nearest rival) had allegedly been telling its suppliers that they would be paid in 120 days, not 90 days. This would severely weaken the suppliers' cash flow position. In addition Halfords allegedly told these suppliers that they must accept a 5% across the range price reduction, and help on the promotion of their products at the retail stage. Monopsony is thus a distorted market, with the buying power so significant that sellers are left with a 'take it or leave it' decision on whether to accept the price the buyer offers.

The care home crisis – an abuse of buying power?

Over the next 25 years the number of over 85s in the UK will double and many in this age group will need care either in specialist homes or in their own home. The increased numbers of elderly people will mean another 18,000 needing care home places compared to today. However, if recent trends continue the number of care home beds will fall by 81,000 by 2020. In 2010 5,190 care home beds were lost and according to a recent report commissioned by BUPA, the health insurance and care provider, this could rise to 8,500 per year by 2015.

Local authorities (mainly county councils) administer adult social care and they purchase beds in care homes on behalf of elderly clients in their jurisdiction. The care home fees are paid by the local authority if clients have low savings, but those with higher savings or with assets such as a house, pay some or all of the fees to the care home. The means tested fees system means that the better off have to pay all of the fees themselves and often have to sell their home to do so. They are said to be 'self funding'.

It seems a little odd that the number of care home beds is going down when the elderly population is increasing. Indeed in January 2011 there were 4,640 delayed discharges of elderly people from NHS hospitals because appropriate care for them could not be arranged. Most of the elderly would like to stay in their own home as long as possible and local authorities support their wishes. Hence, part of the crisis of NHS beds being blocked by the elderly, is the time it takes to arrange what are called packages of care for patients discharged from hospital into their own homes.

It is fair to say that some of the losses in care beds are accounted for by the closure of residential homes resulting from the increased numbers of elderly people continuing to live at home for as long as possible. However, the decline in the number of care home beds is not explained simply by the growth in care provision at home. The fact is making a profit in the privately owned care home sector has become increasingly difficult in recent years. Although there are very large companies in this sector such as Care UK and BUPA Care Homes, who are capable of gaining significant **economies of scale**, even they have struggled. The problem in part is the buying power of local authorities who buy about 60% of beds in care homes on behalf of their clients.

This means that they fix the fees rather than the homes themselves, and care home owners would argue that the fees are not high enough to make a profit. Economists would see the driving down of fees as an abuse of something akin to **monopsony power** by the local authorities. A **monopsonist** is a sole buyer and thus it has huge advantages over the seller. Last April, many local authorities froze the weekly fee per bed leaving care homes with a shortfall/loss on every local authority funded bed of around £90, with £700 the approximate weekly cost per bed. This buying power cannot be explained as an economy of scale where the care homes offer the local authorities discounts for block booking. It seems to be a case of local authorities saying these are our fees - take it or leave it.

Local authorities claim that they have insufficient money to pay any more than they do, although they have recently been given an extra £2bn for adult social care by the central government. However, this money is not ring fenced for care home provision. How do the care homes survive in this situation? Some care homes charge more for self funding clients than they receive for local authority funded clients which in itself is probably anti-competitive and an example of **price discrimination**. There is a possibility of 100,000 elderly people occupying the 170,000 NHS hospital beds in a few years' time if current trends continue. There will simply not be enough care home places to put them when ready for discharge from the NHS hospitals where many are initially admitted. Many would argue that the elderly care problem is too large for the local authorities to handle and that a national care service for the elderly needs to be set up to deal with this complex issue. At the moment it appears to be a ticking time bomb with a slow burning fuse.

Source: Economax tutor2u April 2011.

Question 13.1

Discuss the extent to which the government should intervene to regulate the care home market.

Question 13.2

Distinguish bulk-buying economies of scale from monopsony power.

Unit 14: **Privatisation and regulation**

Privatisation can take a number of forms:

1. Sale of state owned shares in companies. This is the type of privatisation with which the public has become most familiar in recent years.
2. Contracting out of services previously provided by the state, under the process known as compulsory competitive tendering. Examples include school cleaning; refuse collection and council owned leisure centres.
3. The selling of individual state assets such as council houses and government buildings.
4. Deregulation (e.g. of UK bus services in 1986).

When the Conservative government was elected in 1979 it was on a set of radical policies which included extensive privatisation. From 1979 onwards British Telecom, British Gas, British Steel, water supply, electricity distribution, British Airports and railways were just some industries and firms transferred to private ownership. Most privatisations created new PLCs with shareholders buying their stake from the government. These newly privatised firms were thus fully listed companies on the Stock Exchange.

The privatisation of the railways was always very controversial and Railtrack's debts of £3.3bn coupled with an urgent need to raise £2bn led to the government in October 2001 invoking the Railway Act, which put the company into administration. When Railtrack was a PLC there was allegedly a conflict between profit paid to shareholders and new investment. There was always the feeling that safety was compromised in attempting to reduce costs and raise profits. Subsequently **Network Rail** has been created which is a not-for-profit company operated on a commercial basis funded by banks and bondholders.

The Royal Mail, a public limited company wholly owned by the government, has faced many difficulties in recent years with falling letter volumes, intensive competition from firms such as TNT and UK Mail, as well as a huge pension deficit. Royal Mail has seen postal volumes fall by 25% since 2006 as email and text messaging volumes have risen. They are expected to continue to fall 25-40% over the next few years. The Postal Services Act 2011 allows for up to 90% of the business to be sold, with a 10% stake for employees. It is hoped that this will be completed by 2014 with the assets and liabilities of the Royal Mail pension scheme taken over by the government.

The privatisation process in the UK has been complemented by the deregulation or liberalisation of markets in which state owned firms once operated. This involves the removal of barriers that have previously prevented the emergence of competition (the bus industry, financial services and more recently postal services are examples). Where privatisation has not been considered appropriate, as with the NHS, **internal markets** have been created to bring competition. In the NHS, primary healthcare trusts (PCTs) who represent groups of GP's in a geographical area purchase health care from NHS trusts. The NHS internal market continues to be based on a purchaser-provider system, although reforms are on-going with the abolition of PCTs with many of their responsibilities being transferred to clinical commissioning groups made up of GPs and other clinicians. These groups will be given responsibility for spending a significant proportion of the NHS budget in England, and in addition greater competition with the private health sector will be encouraged. Government Ministers believe the reforms included in the Health and Social Care Act 2012 are essential to allow the health service to become more efficient and meet the challenges it is facing. Many health groups, representing NHS employees, have said they oppose the reforms – and these include some royal colleges which set professional standards as well as the major organisations representing doctors, nurses and midwives. With an ageing population and increasing costs of drugs and medical equipment demand on the NHS will surge over the next 20 years and the new reforms are designed to reduce the cost base of the organisation. It is a matter of debate as to whether these reforms form the basis of the partial privatisation of the NHS.

The aims of privatisation

1. **Improving efficiency.** In particular, the former nationalised industries were accused of X-inefficiency. The profit goal, which would now be pursued due to accountability to shareholders, would ensure a drive to eliminate this.

2. **Improving the quality and range of services.** The profit goal, combined with the 'discipline of the market', would lead to the attainment of this target: A high quality, wide-range, of services would be required in order to win custom.

3. **Lower prices.** These would result from competition.

4. **Widening of share ownership.** If more of the labour force become shareholders, it is likely that they will not view the owners of the companies for which they work as capitalists who appropriate the fruits of the labour of the workers. This is because as shareholders they too would be capitalists.

5. **Revenue raising.** The sale of state owned assets and shares deliver a one-off boost to government revenue and therefore a reduction in public sector borrowing.

6. **The creation of companies who, disciplined by the market, would become strong enough to be world leaders, competing on an international scale.**

It is important to note that the achievement of some of these goals is heavily dependent on the measures, complementary to privatisation, to introduce competition. *Ceteris paribus*, the privatisation of a state monopoly creates a private monopoly and exposes the economy to the high prices and inefficient resource allocation that this is likely to entail. However, with the introduction of competition, we have good reason to expect a greater degree of allocative and technical efficiency, together with lower prices. It is partly for this reason that regulatory bodies have been set up to oversee the privatised industries. The aim is to protect the consumer from the potential abuse of monopoly power, and, indeed, from any undesirable side effects of competition. Regulation is particularly important in the water industry where domestic consumers face a regional monopoly.

Has privatisation been successful?

Between 1979 and 1997, the proceeds from privatisation were some £90 billion. Firms which were loss making under public ownership began to make a profit. A study of 33 privatised enterprises found that, prior to privatisation, they absorbed £500 million of public funds annually and £1 billion in loan finance. Although postal services and the rail network continue to receive financial support from the Treasury the privatised firms are no longer the burden they were in the 1970s. The real prices (prices adjusted for inflation) of gas and electricity fell in the 1990s as competition drove down energy bills and much the same occurred in telecommunications. However, there has long been a suspicion that the big six energy companies in the UK are very quick to raise their gas charges to customers when the wholesale gas price rises but very slow to cut charges when the wholesale price falls. The former Energy Secretary Chris Huhne said, when in office, he had concerns that prices to customers had gone "up like a rocket and down like a feather" in response to changes in wholesale prices. Some analysts believed that high UK energy prices were due to **tacit collusion** among the big six suppliers. It has often been asserted that many consumers have failed to benefit from all the price competition in the telecoms and energy markets because they are either unaware that the company they are using is not the cheapest or they cannot be bothered to switch suppliers; the term **customer inertia** is used by economists to describe this phenomenon.

Despite web sites such as www.simplyswitch.com many domestic consumers overpay on their energy bills. Those who have a dual fuel arrangement with their suppler and who pay by direct debit allegedly pay less per unit of energy than those who have separate suppliers or who use pre-payment meters. This could be an example of price discrimination which penalises those on low incomes. Energy suppliers may well point to the lower costs of administering dual fuel accounts made monthly by direct debit. From 1990 to 2011 the average energy bill rose from £530 to £1140, a rise of 115%; while the average water bill rose from £135 to £330, a rise of 144%.

Indeed average annual water bills have risen significantly in real terms since privatisation in 1989 and the period for 2005-2010 saw a similar real terms increase. The price limits set for 2005-2010 meant that the average household customer paid about £46 more in real terms by 2009-2010 than in 2004-05, an increase of around 18%. For the 2010 to 2015 regulatory period many of Britain's water companies wanted to raise annual bills above the level of inflation to fund investment. The increases some of the companies submitted for approval to Ofwat, the water regulator, were as follows:

Southern Water   – Retail Price Inflation + 4.5%
South West Water   – RPI + 3.7%
Thames Water   – RPI + 3.0%
Anglian Water   – RPI + 3.5%
United Utilities   – RPI + 2.0%
Northumbrian Water   – RPI + 1.3%
Yorkshire Water   – RPI + 0.6%

The retail price index figure used by the regulator was based upon the inflation rate for November 2010 which was 4.7%. The biggest increase was sought by Southern Water that wanted to raise bills by retail price inflation plus 4.5 per cent. The company said that this was needed to fund £2.6billion of investment to comply with new European Union environmental regulations.

Changes were made by Ofwat to these proposals with Ofwat for instance allowing South West Water to increase prices at the 4.7% inflation rate plus another 3.4% on top of that to invest in new technology and infrastructure bringing the total up to 8.1%. This is often called an **RPI + K formula** because K represents the allowance for spending on increased investment by the company.

Given these figures it would seem to be very hard to argue against privatisation. However, the collapse of Railtrack and the fact that regulated rail fares have risen in real terms since 1997 indicate that rail privatisation has not been a great success. In addition the standard of service on routes worsened post-privatisation for several years. Although there was a rise in passenger miles travelled after privatisation the rail service was hampered by under-investment, regulatory confusion and an over complex fares structure. However, of late there have been improvements to both rolling stock and track infrastructure as investment has begun to pay off and increasingly trains are arriving on time. There has been substantial investment via the taxpayer in the rail infrastructure, but over the next few years financial support to the rail sector will fall. Pressure on the rail network will continue with the number of rail journeys in Britain at their highest since 1947. More recently the part privatisation of National Air Traffic (NATS) was heavily criticised by the airline industry and trade unions. Privatisation led to huge job losses in the coal, steel and telephone sectors. In addition the desire for wide shareholder ownership among the population has not been achieved to any significant degree. In addition contracting out of public sector services such as hospital cleaning and court security has often led to a decline in quality. Nonetheless further privatisations in the coming years cannot be ruled out (see Question 14.3).

The activities of regulatory bodies

The main functions of regulatory agencies such as Ofwat (water industry) and Ofcom (telecommunications and postal services) and Ofgem (energy) are to control prices in the privatised utility markets, to prevent consumer exploitation and, where necessary, to take account of the existence of externalities. Judging which price level will deliver an efficient resource allocation is thus a difficulty that the regulators face.

Regulators attempt to create the constraints and stimuli which companies experience in a competitive market environment. They thus simulate the effects of competition by price caps and quality standards. Price caps are usually based on a satisfactory rate of profit on the value of assets employed. Performance indicators such as the number of trains that are late or water leakages assess quality standards.

Regulators attempt to encourage competition by easing the entry of new products and preventing privatised firms erecting or maintaining barriers to entry. The regulator will thus promote effective competition and remove market distortions. Legislation now allows regulators to fine companies for breaches of licence conditions. Regulators don't have as much investigative power as the Office of Fair Trading and they can ask the OFT via the Competition Commission to carry out a detailed investigation of possible market abuses such as collusion.

Types of regulation

1. RPI-X

RPI-X means that permitted price increases are determined by the percentage rise in the retail price index (RPI) minus an amount X, where X is the reduction in price required for the industry as a result of expected improvements in efficiency. So for telecoms, between 1997 and 2002 the price formula was RPI – 4.5 per cent (the formula only applied to some customers). This meant that if inflation was 8 per cent, BT would be allowed to raise its prices by only 8% – 4.5% = 3.5%. If inflation was 3 per cent, BT would have to put its price down by 1.5% i.e. 3% – 4.5% = –1.5%. In 2009 regulated rail fares rose by over 6% as the train operators were able to use the July 2008 RPI inflation rate of 5.2% as the basis of their fares structure. These price rises were unpopular with rail users faced with the recession and the credit crunch. Train operators said at the time that the fare increases were necessary to improve the standard of service and these companies felt that if the RPI fell to the extent that retail inflation was negative (deflation) – a possibility during a recession – then fares would have to be cut.

Regulated rail fares will rise by RPI inflation plus 3% for each of the next two years from 2013 as the government seeks to cut the average subsidy per passenger from 30% to 20% and the rail operators seek to improve the standard of service. Not all rail fares are regulated and those which are not often rise by significantly more than RPI + X. For passengers there is also anger that rail fares in Britain are much higher than those in mainland Europe and that it costs up to 30% more to run the railway in Britain than in countries such as Germany and Switzerland.

Figure 14.1: Rail fare increases compared to inflation, %

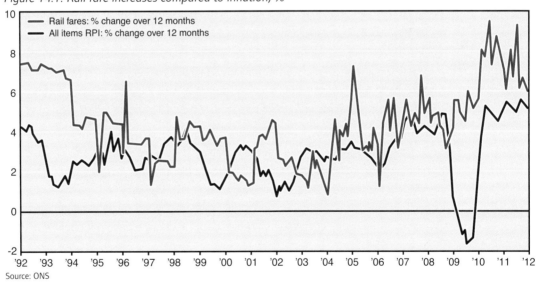

Source: ONS

The problem for the RPI-X system is setting the figure for X. The company needs to provide accurate information about its costs to the regulator but will it? If the regulator sets X too high then the company will have insufficient funds to invest and the standard of service will fall leading to dynamic inefficiency. If X is set too low then excessive profits will be earned. There is also the problem of how long the X factor should be set for. If it's too long then changes in market conditions cannot be taken into account; too short and there is not enough of a time scale for companies to plan ahead with long term investments.

On the other hand RPI-X regulation does give firms the opportunity to plan investment programmes and estimate with some accuracy their revenue streams. For example National Grid has been subject to the

RPI-X regulation for around 20 years. The regulator Ofgem uses price controls to incentivise National Grid to achieve efficiency savings, although a new system of regulation is about to be introduced (see Question 14.4).

Water companies in the UK are regional monopolies, but they have been allowed by their regulator Ofwat to increase real prices using a K factor formula. The K factor is the annual rate by which each licensed water company can increase its charges annually on top of inflation. The K factors are set by Ofwat at a price review, for the next five years. Water companies can defer K, and both Ofwat and the companies can seek interim adjustments of price limits between price reviews. Water companies have been allowed to increase their real prices because of the substantial investment required in new infrastructure and the need to meet environmental standards laid down by the European Union.

The following table illustrates what will happen to average household water bills in the area covered by Southern Water under their business plan for the next regulatory period which was submitted to the regulator Ofwat for approval.

Year	2010/11	2011/12	2012/13	2013/14	2014/15	
	5.3%	3.2%	3.2%	3.0%	0.0%	Average = **2.9%**

In the UK, the water industry price cap formula is sometimes expressed as RPI-X + K. The K is a number determined by the regulator Ofwat every five years for each water company to show what it needs above inflation in order to finance the provision of services to customers. K is an indication of the company's investment requirements which are often related to reducing leaks through infrastructure upgrades as well as meeting EU water purity requirements.

2. Licencing/Franchising

Rail services and the National Lottery are good examples of granting licences or franchises to firms and giving them significant monopoly power. Following the abolition of the Strategic Rail Authority in 2005 the Department of Transport became responsible for the issue of franchises to the Train Operating Companies. There has been much controversy in the rail industry regarding the length of franchises. In the early days after rail privatisation franchises ran for 15 years but they are now often less than half that. The Competition Commission recommended in 2008 that franchises should be at least 12 years with other analysts suggesting 20 years. Short franchises (some have been less than six years) give the train operators little time to plan investment effectively and mean that they are reliant on the train leasing companies. Longer franchises would encourage operators to buy rolling stock which lasts 20 years or more.

Until recently most rail franchises currently ran for seven or eight years and Association of Train Operating Companies have always wanted franchises to have a standard length of fifteen years. However, in 2010 the government announced that there would be a standard rail franchise length of 10 years with the possibility extending it to more than 20 years. This change was supported by the rail sector because it gives train operators more time to invest in and profit from new rolling stock, although operators face big financial penalties if they don't complete a franchise because they are finding it unprofitable.

The National Lottery Commission, the regulator, announced in 2007 that Camelot was to be appointed as the operator to run The National Lottery from 2009-2019. Camelot has operated the National Lottery since its inception in 1994. The licence to run the lottery carries with it numerous conditions and Camelot must stay within its licence or risk fines or other punishment. However, the firm does have a legalised monopoly similar to the train operating companies such as First Great Western and Virgin Trains. If the length of the franchise is set correctly for the industry licensing brings together the benefits of competition (in the bidding process) with those of a natural monopoly.

3. Rate of return regulation

This form of regulation includes the regulator setting what it thinks is a 'normal' rate of return on the capital employed in the business. This rate of return is set higher than the interest paid to acquire the capital. The government then taxes at 100% any profit made above this 'normal' rate. The problem for this form of regulation is that firms have no incentive to be efficient beyond a certain level. If they work very hard to improve efficiency and raise their profits as a consequence they will find these extra profits taxed away as a result of all their efforts!

Rate of return regulation also has the problem that it encourages firms to overvalue their assets. If they are allowed to make a 10% return on their assets then it would be in their financial interests to falsely value them at £100m than at the correct figure of say £75m. A 10% return on £100m is £10m and far better than £7.5m.

4. Yardstick competition

Sometimes the regulator uses the performance of different firms in the industry to set price and customer service standards. It is used when the firms are regionally separate and there may be no direct competition, such as exists with the UK water authorities. The best performing firms thus set the standard and are used as a yardstick for the rest of the industry when a price regime is formulated. In theory it is possible for the regulator to use yardstick competition to maximise efficiency and eliminate abnormal profits when cost changes across firms are analysed. However, the precise way in which comparative cost information is used in price reviews by regulators such as Ofwat is often unclear and sometimes comparisons appear to be subjective. Geographical, climatic and geological differences between the water regions make this difficult.

Judging the effectiveness of regulation

These questions could be asked when assessing the success of a regulator.

1. What has been the effect of regulation on:
   - real prices to customers?
   - levels of competition in the industry?
   - employment and productivity levels in the industry?
   - the quality of service?
   - investment levels in the industry?

2. How far has the regulator been able to adapt to changes in market conditions and technology? i.e. from monitoring the performance of a single firm towards assessing the performance of a competitive market as a whole.

3. To what extent will the regulator be able to bring about market conditions, which reduce its role to relatively minor issues? The regulator initially acts in place of competition in a monopolistic market; will it be able to make itself redundant in time?

How successful has regulation been in the UK?

The regulator is there to encourage competition in an industry that may have been privatised as a monopoly. If there is no competition, possibly because the industry is a natural monopoly then the regulator's duty is to make the firm act as though they were operating in a competitive market. Once there is competition in the market the regulator has to consider the prices charged by firms and the quality of service they provide. Regulators will also seek to reduce barriers to entry to the market, such as the pressure placed on BT in recent years by Ofcom to open up the 'local loop' in its line infrastructure to other telecoms firms so that they can provide telephone and internet services. This led to the creation of a separate company, Openreach.

The UK regulators were given industry structures to work with, post privatisation, some were good others not so good. The initial fall in real prices in gas, electricity and telecoms was encouraging but the consumer has paid for the massive investment needed in the water infrastructure through higher water bills. In time increased competition will replace many aspects of regulation, but many markets will remain dominated by a few large firms and the electricity and gas infrastructure will remain a natural monopoly, as will water quite probably. In addition even when a market is competitive firms may fail to take into account environmental or social objectives.

The RPI-X formula can potentially lead to huge improvements in efficiency but has the regulator always been dealing with accurate information when setting price controls? How easy is it to set the value of X? However, regulators are independent and do not have to answer to the government or the firms involved. With their specialist knowledge it can be argued that they are the best people to decide whether the firms in an industry are acting in the public interest. Regulators have a long term future in these markets despite the increase in competition. There may appear to be a competitive market but regulators may find that the market may not be working effectively, a view that many felt applied to the UK energy market in 2008 when it was investigated by Ofgem.

Clearly some of the UK privatisations could have created better structures in their markets, this may be particularly true of rail and energy. Consequently the regulation of these industries has been difficult at times. In the rail sector it has been argued that the train leasing companies (ROSCOs) have made huge abnormal profits largely at the expense of passengers. ROSCOs lease the rolling stock to train operating companies such as Virgin and First Great Western. However, as markets evolve regulation has to adapt and in energy a new system is being created as the UK energy sector has to respond to emissions targets and the closure of old coal fired power stations. Energy generation and transmission require significant investment over the coming years and regulation will need to reflect these changes.

Regulatory capture

Regulatory bodies are often accused of being too soft on the businesses that they control, which are still making huge profits. The issue of regulatory capture (where the regulator starts to serve the interests of the monopolists rather than limit their power) has often been raised. While there is little evidence to support the claim that this is happening, it remains likely that firms are able to influence regulators to some degree. Regulatory capture was possibly a reason why the electricity industry was able to enjoy a very lax regulatory regime from Offer (the then electricity regulator) in the mid-1990's. In 1998 Peter Davis, the head of OFLOT the then lottery regulator, resigned after it emerged that he accepted free flights from GTech, the parent company of Camelot, who run the UK's lottery. However, some regulators have taken a strong independent view and Tom Winsor in charge of the Office of Rail Regulation until 2004 was forthright in his criticism of government policy towards the railways in the UK, and had a stormy relationship with Railtrack (prior to it becoming Network Rail). There have also been accusations of weak or ineffective regulation by the Civil Aviation Authority (CAA) with regard to British airports (mainly BAA) and also by the Financial Services Authority (FSA) in the banking sector. Whether these two examples amount to regulatory capture is more debateable. The key issue is the ability of the regulator to gain all the information they need from the firms and to act on it effectively in the interests of all stakeholders (customers, investors, and the firms themselves). Regulators do not have the same investigative powers as the Competition Commission.

Question 14.1

(a) Using examples explain what is meant by a natural monopoly?

(b) How should a natural monopoly be regulated?

Question 14.2

RPI-X price regulation has been around 25 years – is it still fit for purpose?

Written by: Roger Barnard, 23 January 2009 (Source: Utility Week)

Roger Barnard says Ofgem should be wary of some of the easy answers being bandied about as it explores alternatives to RPI-X regulation. There are markets in ideas, just as there are markets in soya beans and shares. Price controls on the RPI-X incentive model were first implemented during the utility privatisations of the 1980s. They were seen as the best alternative to the direct regulation of dividends and profits. The policy objectives were to improve the efficiency and productivity of regulated companies, and to keep prices low to the consumer.

This model has since been evolved by regulators into a much more complex scheme of control over the activities and outputs of the network-based utilities that provide the basic infrastructure of modern life. But all markets overshoot, and even the best ideas can be pushed to their logical conclusion – and beyond. A big unanswered question for the utility industries, therefore, is whether RPI-X remains a stock worth holding.

Ofgem, the gas and electricity regulator thinks this question is so important that it has set up a two-year project – the 'RPI-X at 20' review – to investigate the workings of the current approach. The review will report back with recommendations to Ofgem's governing body, the Gas and Electricity Markets Authority, in summer 2010. Its aim is to ascertain if the RPI-X model is still fit for purpose or whether, after two decades of incremental development, the regulatory framework needs more fundamental change.

Actually, Ofgem ought to have called its project the 'RPI-X at 25' review, since it is now a quarter of a century since Stephen Littlechild produced his hugely influential report for the former Department of Industry on how to regulate British Telecom's pricing after privatisation. Littlechild advocated a pseudo-competitive mechanism, in which the regulated company would be both incentivised to outperform the cost assumptions of the price control and allowed to retain the benefit of the resulting efficiency gains. This laid the foundation for the RPI-X regimes that are now in force for almost all of the monopoly industries in the utilities sector.

Admiration

However, the admiration we all must have for Littlechild's great contribution to the practice of utility price regulation should not sway Ofgem from moving on. Regulatory agencies rarely question the fundamental basis of what they are doing. Inertia inside the structures of regulation, as in all fields of public administration, means that officials prefer to soldier on until a crisis erupts, at which point the available solutions are likely to be sub-optimal. So Ofgem is to be commended for conducting a review of potentially great significance, not just for the energy industry but for the utilities sector as a whole.

Two recent public workshops sponsored by Ofgem were quick to identify the key issue for the review. It is whether the RPI-X model of fixed-term price caps can continue to deliver an equitable settlement between customers and owners, while enabling gas and electricity networks to invest to meet the new security of supply and carbon reduction objectives at the heart of current energy policy. This is a debate of great national importance, and the issues with which the review will need to engage are both numerous and difficult. Here are four candidates for Ofgem's urgent attention.

First, the fashionable idea that some of the complexity of price controls can be replaced by a simpler process, in which customer groups negotiate directly with companies on the key parameters of a settlement, should be treated with caution. The recent ruling by the Competition Commission that BAA acted against the public interest in failing to 'engage constructively' with airline companies about its investment plans for a second Stansted runway is clearly significant. But merely to mention this case is to highlight the fact that, in energy, there is no obvious counterparty for network operators to agree settlements with. Suppliers cannot fulfil that role because network operators have statutory duties and they do not. That is why the proxy for the customer is the regulator – Ofgem.

Negotiated settlements

The parallels that are being drawn with the use of negotiated settlements overseas are also unhelpful. While it is true that negotiated price caps are possible under some state jurisdictions in America and Canada, these are an adjunct to the normal method of regulation and are made possible only through a well-defined legal framework.

This is the reverse of the situation in Britain, where the rules and standards of regulatory process are poorly defined and decision-making is often subjective and always unpredictable from one price control period to the next. In this context, negotiated settlements, far from simplifying

regulation, are likely to bring even further complexity into the picture, and to result in a patchwork system of second-best outcomes.

An issue that may need greater visibility in the review is the industry's operational and financial resilience. Looking back with the benefit of hindsight, it can be seen that the evolution of the price control methodology over two decades has reflected a particularly narrow view of efficiency held by economic regulators. The real-world consequences of this have been networks that are more capacity constrained and generally older than they should be, and investment decisions that tend to be dominated by fear of regulatory disallowance. A just-in-time approach to asset renewal and enhancement leads to lower levels of industry resilience and, over time, may ultimately put whole systems at risk of catastrophic failure.

Cost shocks

The same may also be true of the potential for external cost shocks, or other adverse economic events, to produce financial distress for network operators, especially those in group structures that are highly debt-leveraged. Gas and electricity networks are primary public goods. The scale of collateral social damage in the event of any systemic failure of an energy infrastructure provider is almost incalculable.

Luckily, as a recent position paper from Ofgem points out, the financial ring-fencing and special administration regimes for regulated energy assets have never had to be tested to destruction. But we should note that, in the implosion of banking systems over the past 18 months, regulators were at all times behind the curve, not ahead of it, and every important regulatory safeguard, both structural and behavioural, failed.

With tighter credit markets, regulated companies could have more difficulty in future in attracting capital for network investment needs. A sharper focus on ex ante measures to avoid the risk of operational or financial failure may result in a more prescriptive regulatory approach to output delivery and companies' capital structures. The greater the degree of prescription, the more important it will be for the price control process to provide adequate checks and balances for licensees. So a third issue for early attention, as you might expect from a lawyer trespassing on economists' territory, is that Ofgem should include legislative change within the scope of its review.

General concern

This issue is of general concern for utility industries. There are generic statutory provisions in place across the sector, which enable the Competition Commission to act in effect as an appeals body against price control determinations for regulated companies. The fact that there has been no reference of a disputed price control proposal for the energy industry for more than ten years strongly suggests that companies feel deterred from making use of the appeals process in the way that Parliament intended.

This is hardly surprising because, under the current system of appeal, the Competition Commission re-examines all of the issues in order to reach a fresh determination, and the company has little or no control over the terms of reference (which can be significant). A better system would be for a company to have to specify the items of difference between itself and the regulator, with the commission being required to decide in favour of one side or the other on each such item, rather like pendulum arbitration in industrial disputes. This approach – which would require new legislation – would strengthen the incentive on the regulator to ensure that its decision on each component of the methodology was correct.

A final concern is the leisurely pace of this review. Originally announced in March last year, its conclusions – which could be radical – will not be available until late in 2010, and the earliest that any major changes of approach could take effect in a price control would be the electricity transmission settlement scheduled for spring 2012. This generous timeframe, covering four years from inception to implementation, seems dangerously inconsistent with the urgency of the new national policy demands on the energy networks industry.

It is right to remind ourselves that models of regulation should not be changed without good reason, not least because of the importance of regulatory stability. Of course there must be consultation, and of course it must be detailed and extensive. But as we rightly celebrate its 25th anniversary, let us not forget that Stephen Littlechild's ground-breaking report on economic regulation was produced and submitted to the government of the day in just six weeks – and that included the Christmas holiday.

Roger Barnard is a barrister and the head of regulatory law at EDF Energy. This article contains his personal views.

Question: Evaluate the UK experience of RPI-X regulation.

Question 14.3

The privatisation of Royal Mail – first of many?

Beginning soon after she took office in 1979 with the first stage sell-off of British Petroleum, Margaret Thatcher's privatisation programme accelerated in the 1980s with the successive sales of utility companies in industries such as electricity, gas and water. In recent years privatisation has slipped off the political and economic radar although it has occasionally reached the news with the possible part privatisation of the Royal Mail and also the sale of The Tote.

With the election of a new coalition government privatisation has risen up the political agenda again partly because of the huge fiscal deficit. The proceeds from any privatisations will help the government finances as well as offer the opportunity for private capital to improve performance.

The first and most important privatisation is likely to be the Royal Mail which has huge problems which stem from the decline in the number of letters being posted as well as Royal Mail's declining share of this shrinking market. This is partly the result of the popularity of email and text messaging and the competition Royal Mail faces from firms such as TNT and UK Mail in the bulk mail market. Given that Royal Mail depends on letters for 80% of its business this would be bad enough. However, the Royal Mail also has a huge pension deficit of over £8bn.

The most recent of many government plans to guide the Royal Mail to a stable financial future (its letters business lost £333m last year) were announced in the autumn of 2010. The coalition plans to privatise most of the Royal Mail apart from the Post Office network which will remain in the public sector. The Royal Mail needs new investment and a reform of working practices if it is to survive, and offering employees 10% of the shares may possibly take away some of the expected trade union opposition to the privatisation of the business.

It is quite possible that the privatisation programme will not stop with the Royal Mail. Many Conservatives see the extension of the privatisation programme as a 'get out of jail free' card for a government which is desperate to repair the public finances. There is a long list of possible privatisation targets which include Radio 1, The Tote, the Dartford Crossing, British Waterways, the Metrological Office, the Forestry Commission, BBC Worldwide, Channel 4 and the entire UK motorway system. Some on this list have been put in the shop window before, especially The Tote which is the state owned bookmaker.

The problem has been, and probably will be, whether the government gets a good price for these assets. In difficult economic times and the knowledge among investors that the government needs to raise money urgently will possibly make this a buyers market with the assets being sold on the cheap. Of equal importance will these assets be better off in private sector ownership? British Waterways and the Forestry Commission do produce external benefits in their present form – would market forces and the profit motive reduce the benefits these bodies at present give to society? For instance the Forestry Commission's forests have become a massive recreational asset, offering a

general freedom to roam not available on private land. Simply because access is so open, nobody knows precisely how many people enjoy the state-owned forests, but the commission's own estimate is that they receive more than 50 million visits a year from walkers, joggers, picnickers, campers, caravaners etc.

The coalition government will need to take a close look at what the government owns and what it needs to own in the future. However, that is a difficult issue to resolve because the USA, a strong argument for private enterprise and free markets, still has a rail and postal system owned by the state. It is a question of what type of mixed economy the UK wants and getting the right balance between the public and private sector.

Reproduced by kind permission of tutor2u from their online magazine Economax.

Question: What are the disadvantages of the possible privatisations mentioned in the above passage?

Question 14.4

Because price control mechanisms restrict revenues, not profits, they encourage efficiencies within our regulated businesses. Savings that are made can be retained for the remainder of the price control period, but the higher level of efficiency that led to these savings is then used to inform a new baseline level for the next price control period.

Price control regulation is designed to ensure that, as a monopoly, we charge reasonable prices, and to provide us with a future level of revenue sufficient to enable us to meet our statutory duties and licence obligations. It also provides financial incentives to manage and operate our networks in an economic, efficient and coordinated manner in accordance with our legal and licence obligations, offer good quality of service to network users and invest in our networks in a timely and efficient manner to help ensure long-term security of supply is maintained.

During each price control review period, the amount of money that can be earned by our regulated businesses is restricted by what is referred to as an RPI-X price control, which is normally reviewed every five years by Ofgem. The RPI-X allowance is based upon Ofgem's estimates of efficient operating expenditure, capital expenditure and asset replacement, together with an allowance for depreciation and an allowed rate of return on capital invested in our businesses. This is summarised in the diagram below, representing a building block model of the price control.

Building blocks

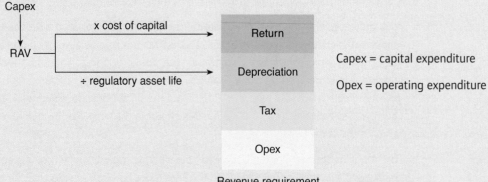

The inputs of the building block model are used, together with the **regulatory asset base value** (RAV) to calculate the allowed revenue. The RAV, which represents the value ascribed by Ofgem to the capital employed in our regulated businesses, is adjusted to reflect asset additions, removals, depreciation and the rate of inflation.

The RPI-X price control takes the retail price index as its benchmark and subtracts X, an efficiency factor, from it. For example, at a time when annual inflation was 3%, a value for X of 2% would allow our regulatory businesses to raise prices by no more than 1%. Price controls also include incentive mechanisms to encourage us to improve our performance in particular areas.

The price control provides our regulated businesses with a level of revenue that is sufficient to finance the businesses if they are efficiently run. The revenue allowance is based on an estimate of the costs an efficient company would face in running its regulated businesses and includes operating expenditure, capital expenditure, financing costs including both debt and equity, and taxation.

Current price controls

The key elements of the current price controls for both gas and electricity transmission are that we are allowed to earn a 4.4% post-tax real return on our RAV, equivalent to a 5.05% vanilla return, with a £4.4 billion baseline five year capex allowance and a £1.2 billion five year controllable opex allowance.

In addition, we are subject to a number of incentives that can adjust our transmission network revenue. For electricity transmission, these include incentives for network reliability, sulphur hexafluoride losses, efficiency and balancing services. For gas transmission, our incentive schemes cover areas such as the cost of investment for additional capacity to facilitate new connections to the system.

The key elements of the current price controls for gas distribution are that we are allowed to earn a 4.3% post-tax real rate of return on our RAV, equivalent to a 4.94% vanilla return, with a £2.5 billion baseline five year capex allowance and a £1.6 billion five year controllable opex allowance.

	RAV	Return on equity
Electricity transmission	£8,388m	13.6%
Gas transmission	£4,889m	15.8%
Gas distribution	£7,520m	12.1%
Total	£20,797m	13.6%

Ofgem's review of price controls: RPI–X@20

Since privatisation, the RPI-X mechanism has provided the industry with strong incentives to be more efficient. The level of opex costs has decreased over the years, transforming previously inefficient nationalised industries. However, over the past few years new challenges, such as Great Britain's transition to lower carbon emissions and the requirement to renew ageing networks, have caused Ofgem to review the continuing appropriateness of the RPI-X approach. In March 2008, Ofgem announced the RPI-X@20 review, which was a two year project to review the workings of the current approach to regulating Great Britain's energy networks and develop future policy recommendations.

Ofgem's RPI-X@20 review aims were to: drive improvements in quality of service and efficiency; ensure that the regulatory framework is flexible to adapt to structural changes in the energy industry; and enable efficient network companies to finance themselves efficiently. To allow the lessons of the review to be accommodated in full, Ofgem extended the current transmission price control from its scheduled end in March 2012 by one year to March 2013. Following the RPI-X@20 review, Ofgem has identified a modified price control approach, designated as RIIO, to deliver and meet the changing future needs of the energy market. RIIO stands for revenue, incentives, innovation and outputs.

Reproduced by the kind permission of National Grid PLC

Question: Investigate how RIIO will work in electricity transmission.

Unit 15: **Competition policy in the UK and the European Union**

Because of the link between competition and efficiency suggested by economic theory, competition authorities (in the UK the main bodies are the Office of Fair Trading and the Competition Commission) are charged with preventing the abuse of monopoly power and guarding against restrictive practices. Restrictive, or anti-competitive, practices are those undertaken by a firm with a view to limiting competition in its markets. Predatory pricing is a prime example. The competition authorities in the UK will investigate activities, which prevent, restrict or distort competition.

Office of Fair Trading

The aim of the Office of Fair Trading (OFT) is to make markets work better for consumers. It does this through the enforcement of competition law and consumer protection law and also by investigating markets where competition does not appear to be working effectively. The OFT will often examine market situations where the market structure or the actions of firms restrict, distort or prevent competition. Sometimes the OFT will carry out all of the investigation itself but in the case of mergers and certain market situations the OFT will complete an initial investigation and if there is enough evidence to suggest a threat to competition the matter will be referred to the Competition Commission.

Competition Commission

The Competition Commission has the responsibility for the detailed investigation into merger, market and regulatory issues referred to it by the OFT and regulators such as OFCOM. Derek Morris, a former chairman of the Commission, said rather controversially in 2002 that profitability would be a key factor in assessing mergers. He said, "Where you find the main players in a market all seem to be consistently making high profits that are one signal that maybe the market is not competitive". The Enterprise Act, which came into force in 2003, took the final decisions on the approval of mergers out of the hands of government ministers and made the Competition Commission responsible for approving or rejecting mergers and setting out potential remedies. However, the **Competition Appeal Tribunal** is an appeals process for interested parties to challenge OFT decisions.

According to the Competition Commission web site they investigate and address issues of concern in three areas:

- Mergers – when the proposed merged company supplies at least 25 per cent of the UK market (this is known as the share of supply test) and the value of UK turnover of the enterprise which is being acquired exceeds £70 million (this known as 'the turnover test'). The proposed merger may then pose a threat to competition in one or more markets.

- Markets – when it appears that competition may be being prevented, distorted or restricted in a particular market (for example its investigation into airport ownership dominated by British Airports Authority – BAA).

- Regulated sectors – where aspects of the regulatory system may not be operating effectively or to address certain categories of dispute between regulators and regulated companies. In 2011 the regulator Ofgem told the six major energy companies that they must offer simpler tariffs to help consumers compare prices. The regulator argued that competition in the UK energy market was being stifled through complicated tariffs and a lack of transparency. Ofgem warned the firms that they could be referred to the Competition Commission if they do not comply with the new system. The UK competition authorities have significant powers to investigate suspected anti-competitive behaviour (including entering and searching business and private premises with a warrant) and to impose fines on businesses found to have infringed competition law. Criminal proceedings are also possible for the most serious breaches of competition law.

The Office of Fair Trading and the Competition Commission will be merged under plans by the coalition government to cut costs. Under the proposed changes, the new body will still have responsibility for investigating company mergers, cartels and issues of unfair market dominance, but much of the work the two bodies do on consumer protection will be moved elsewhere, possibly to the trading standard divisions of local authorities. The merger of the two will bring the UK competition system into line with many other western countries that have a single-body model. There is general support for the move as businesses often complain that investigations take too long, sometimes at least a year at the OFT followed by a further two years at the Competition Commission. Even then there is an appeals process for decisions to be challenged. It has also been felt that here has always been an element of duplication between the two.

Alongside the amalgamation of the OFT and the Competition Commission new powers for the new body, the **Competition and Markets Authority**, have been announced. Under new rules, prosecutors will not have to prove 'dishonest participation' in criminal cartels before an offence is committed. It is hoped that this will make it easier for the new body to successfully prosecute individuals in criminal cases when they have set up cartels. In recent years the OFT has been very unsuccessful in criminal prosecutions.

The Takeover Panel

While the OFT and the Competition Commission are concerned with wider public interest issues the Takeover Panel is concerned with the fair conduct of a takeover bid from the point of view of shareholders when a change in control of companies is possible. The Takeover Panel was set up in 1968 to protect the interests of shareholders of public companies involved in a merger whether they are listed on the Stock Exchange or unlisted. It is concerned with the process of a merger rather than its desirability.

The controversial takeover of Cadbury by Kraft in 2010 raised concerns that UK firms were easy targets for takeover by foreign firms. There was talk of raising the takeover for a successful bid to 75% from 50% approval of the shareholding. The UK Takeover Code was substantially amended in 2011 with a view to addressing the perceived imbalance in UK takeovers between target companies and bidders in hostile situations. The most significant change in the revised Code was to the "put up or shut up" regime. This meant that not only must a prospective bidder now be publicly named in any announcement by the target firm at the beginning of an offer period, but thereafter it now has only 28 days either to launch a bid, or walk away and be prevented from making an offer for at least six months. Bidders must also reveal details of their financing and advisory fees.

Mergers policy

The **Fair Trading Act (1973)** states that any merger or acquisition involving more than a 25% market share in the UK or involves assets of more than £70m world wide is eligible for referral to the Competition Commission. At least one of the firms must operate in the UK. The Office of Fair Trading decides whether the merger is referred for a Competition Commission investigation. The Competition Commission has to decide whether the merger is in the 'public interest'. The following issues have to be considered when trying to assess the 'public interest'.

● Maintaining and promoting competition in the UK.

● Promoting the interests of consumers.

● Promoting new products and reducing costs.

● Maintaining and promoting the balanced distribution of industry and employment.

● Maintaining and promoting competitive activity in overseas markets by companies in the UK.

New legislation in the **Enterprise Act (2002)** shifted the emphasis of assessing a merger away from the 'public interest' and towards considering what it does to competition. The Act also prevents ministers overruling Competition Commission decisions on acquisitions/mergers. The Enterprise Act has revolutionised the UK's competition law and strengthened the Competition Commission's place as the authority to which complex merger cases and investigations into abuses of market power are referred by the OFT. Since the Enterprise Act the number of merger cases referred to the Competition Commission has risen significantly.

In 2010 the OFT and the Competition Commission introduced new merger guidelines which are designed to assist companies by providing greater clarity on how the competitive impact of mergers is assessed by the two bodies. These guidelines built upon those published after the introduction of the Enterprise Act 2002. The guidelines set out the questions the OFT and Competition Commission will consider when reviewing mergers, how they define a "relevant merger situation" and what is meant by a "substantial lessening of competition".

Monopoly policy

The Office of Fair Trading (OFT) could investigate any firm thought to be abusing market power locally or nationally. The OFT has to investigate whether the firm has a dominant market position. Very often firms will not be investigated if their market share is less than 40%. The OFT will look at the contestability of the market the firm is operating in and whether it is engaging in anti-competitive practices. If the firm is found to be abusing its market position fines of up to 10% of turnover can be imposed by the OFT.

The Competition Commission investigated the UK groceries sector in 2009. The key areas of concern were the behaviour of grocery retailers towards their suppliers (the buying power of supermarkets); the structure of any local market for groceries (localised monopolies or duopolies); and land and planning issues (supermarkets holding banks of land that they refuse to sell to possible competitors thereby raising barriers to entry). These issues potentially restrict, distort and prevent competition.

In recent years a major investigation by the Competition Commission into abuse of monopoly power has involved the UK airport owner British Airports Authority (BAA). Owned by Spanish firm Ferrovial, BAA originally operated Heathrow, Gatwick, Southampton and Aberdeen, as well as Stansted, Glasgow and Edinburgh. In March 2009, the Competition Commission told BAA to sell Gatwick and Stansted airports and either Edinburgh or Glasgow. BAA has already sold Gatwick but challenged the decision to sell the other airports. BAA lost its appeal against the sale of Stansted Airport at the Competition Appeal Tribunal in 2012 but was subsequently allowed to make its case at the Court of Appeal against the original Competition Commission ruling.

Restrictive practices policy

Cartels and other restrictive practices are illegal under the **1998 Competition Act**. Prior to this Act the OFT would only force firms to abandon such practices. Since the Act came into force firms can be fined up to 10% of annual turnover for every year they engage in restrictive practices (up to a maximum of 3 years). The Enterprise Act (2002) meant that not only can firms be fined but also directors can be disqualified and imprisoned. When British Airways (BA) and Virgin were found guilty of fixing fuel surcharges on long haul passenger flights between 2004 and 2006 BA were fined £121.5m by the OFT. The OFT then brought a criminal prosecution against four BA executives which can mean fines and a jail sentence of up to five years. However, the case collapsed in 2010 when the OFT withdrew its case against the British Airways executives on trial. In a criminal case a much higher burden of proof is required than in a civil action as evidenced in this case with the court spending months hearing arguments about whether and how price fixing should be a criminal offence. The OFT is able at present to enter business premises and search for incriminating evidence of collusion which is often difficult to identify. The OFT is concerned to investigate any activity which they think restricts, distorts or prevents competition, and now will pay up to £100,000 to anyone who provides them with information which provides evidence of anti-competitive practices among firms. The 1998 Competition Act states that any activity, which threatens to 'appreciably' reduce the level of competition in an industry, could be investigated.

Examples of anti-competitive practice include:

1. **Predatory pricing** and **limit pricing**.

2. **Restriction of supply** to distributors.

3. **'Full-line forcing'.** The retailer is forced to stock the complete range of a manufacturer's products; otherwise he will not be supplied at all. This leaves little room for stocking competitors to the range. A variation on this theme, investigated by the competition authorities, is the practice of 'freezer exclusivity' employed by Bird Eye Walls (BEW) in its attempt to fight off Mars ice cream in the 1990's. BEW loaned freezer

A retailer may be forced to stock a manufacturer's complete range.

cabinets to many retailers who stock its entire range and sought to prevent retailers stocking the products of rivals in those cabinets, a policy that was likely to be particularly successful given that many retail outlets do not have sufficient floor space for more than one cabinet. In 2004, the European Union (EU) Competition Commission investigated a similar case with Coca-Cola. Following a complaint by PepsiCo, Coke's smaller rival, an agreement was reached which meant that Coca-Cola allowed up to 20% of the shelf space in its fridges to be used to stock drinks from competitor firms. The agreement applied in all EU countries where Coca-Cola had a market share of over 40%.

4. Creation of **artificial barriers to entry**, through activities such as extremely high advertising expenditure or wide-ranging brand proliferation.

Examples of collusive restrictive practice include:

5. **Market sharing, collusive tendering** and **price fixing/cartels**.

6. Agreements on types of goods to be produced or to co-ordinate investment.

Collusive behaviour involving more than 25% of the market is likely to be investigated although price fixing agreements, which have a dramatic effect at a local level, could also be eligible. In recent years a number of high profile cartel cases have featured the leniency applied to former cartel members who 'blow the whistle' on others. Although a controversial policy, whistle blowers do save the competition authorities a lot of time and the possibility of immunity from prosecution can be seen as a way of weakening cartels. A notable example was Virgin escaping prosecution when it volunteered details to the OFT of its price fixing cartel with BA over fuel surcharges between 2004 and 2006.

Assessment of UK competition policy

The Competition Act (1998) and the **Enterprise Act (2002)** have brought UK legislation more closely in line with European Union competition policy and the new legislation has shifted the focus to anti-competitive practices and their effects rather than on agreements and the size of a firm's market share. The OFT and Competition Commission now places more emphasis on the contestability of markets rather than the assumption that structure determines conduct and performance. Mergers were not covered by the 1998 Act which means that there is no presumption that a merger is against the public interest, the Competition Commission has to prove this. Most mergers are not referred to the Commission and there is

plenty of evidence that many are not in the public interest. However, the recent legislation has given the OFT and the Competition Commission much more power; imposing fines, entering and searching businesses, and independence from the government. The post-1997 Labour government was very keen to see greater competition in all UK markets and is part of their commitment to improve the performance of the UK economy.

Competition Appeal Tribunal

The Competition Appeal Tribunal was created by the Enterprise Act 2002. The current functions of the Tribunal are to hear appeals with respect to decisions made by the OFT under the Competition Act 1998. When a case is heard The Tribunal consists of three members. The panel of chairmen are judges of the Chancery Division of the High Court and other senior lawyers. The ordinary members of the Tribunal have expertise in law, business, accountancy, economics and other related fields. British Airports Authority appealed to the Tribunal following the Competition Commission ruling that it should sell Stansted Airport. The appeal was rejected by the Tribunal in 2011.

In September 2009 the OFT fined 103 construction companies £129.5m over allegations of collusion on contract bidding between 2000 and 2006 which then pushed up the price of building contracts. The Competition Appeal Tribunal said the fines were "excessive given the nature of the infringement" and cut them from £41.8m for six companies to just £4.4m. Many experts believed that this judgement cast doubt over how the OFT calculates fines.

Question 15.1

(a) Bus market not competitive enough

In January 2010 the OFT referred Britain's bus industry to the Competition Commission. The big five bus companies, FirstGroup, Stagecoach, National Express, Go-Ahead and Arriva account for about two thirds of the local bus market outside London and that the local transport authorities were predominantly served by just one bus company. The OFT believed that there was insufficient competition in the market with bus fares 9% higher where there is very little competition on routes. The established bus operators were also allegedly prone to predatory pricing against new entrants.

In addition the OFT felt that the large bus operators respected each other's geographical territories too much for fear of igniting a price war. Local bus services in recent years have received £1.2 billion annual government subsidies and the OFT wanted the Competition Commission to see if taxpayers were getting value for money. Not surprisingly the bus companies claimed the investigation was a distraction and a waste of time and money.

Investigate the findings of the Competition Commission.
http://www.bbc.co.uk/news/business-16261086

(b) Big four auditors face competition probe

Four large companies dominate the audit market- these are firms which audit the accounts of major PLCs. The four companies are Price Waterhouse Coopers, KPMG, Deloitte and Ernst and Young. In 2010 the OFT found that 99% of audit fees paid by the FTSE100 companies went to the big four and between 2002 and 2010 only 2.3% of these companies switched auditor. Between them the major firms audit all but one of Britain's FTSE100 companies and all but ten of the FTSE250. The OFT felt that high entry barriers, high levels of market concentration and an apparent lack of competition justified an investigation by the Competition Commission which the OFT initiated in late 2011.

Investigate the progress of this investigation.
http://www.bbc.co.uk/news/business-15412744

European Union competition policy

The European Union (EU) is becoming increasingly significant with regard to UK competition policy. EU law allows for penalties of up to 10 per cent of turnover, where evidence of anti-competitive behaviour is found. This is the same as in the UK. The EU traditionally left such matters to individual member states, unless there is an appreciable effect on trade between members. Following the **Single European Act (1987)** and the subsequent creation of the single market in 1992, the number of cases covered by this criterion has inevitably increased, with EU investigations in areas such as telecommunications, energy and transport services. Sir Leon Brittan, an EU Commissioner at the time, hailed an agreement, shortly after the Act, to give the EU broader competition policy powers as "unquestionably an historic breakthrough for the EU in the context of the single European market. There can be no internal market without a common competition policy."

The European Union thus has rules to ensure free competition in the Single Market. The **European Commission** is responsible for applying these rules throughout the Community, working closely with national governments. The EU competition rules were set out in **Article 86**, **Article 81** and **Article 82** of the Treaty of Rome.

Article 87 of the EC Treaty prohibits any aid granted by a member state or through state resources in any form whatsoever which distorts or threatens to distort competition by favouring certain firms or the production of certain goods. The aid in question can take a variety of forms for instance: government grants or interest relief and tax relief.

Article 81 prohibits anti-competitive agreements, which may have an appreciable effect on trade between Member States and which prevent, restrict or distort competition in the Single Market. The Commission can grant individual or group exemptions from this prohibition if there are overriding countervailing benefits such as an improvement in efficiency or the promotion of research and development. **Article 82** prohibits the abuse of a dominant position insofar as it may affect trade between member states. There is no possibility of exemption. Abuse of dominant position was the centrepiece of a long running battle between the EU Competition Commission and Microsoft. The Commission fined Microsoft €497 million because by bundling up Windows Media Player with its Windows operating system Microsoft had damaged rival media players' ability to compete.

The European Commission will consider investigating a merger, which creates a dominant position as a result of which effective competition would be significantly impeded in the common market or in a substantial part of it. The Regulation applies to all mergers with a 'Community dimension', defined by reference to turnover criteria.

In 2011 the European Commission blocked a proposed merger between Greece's Olympic Air and Aegean Airlines saying that it would create a "quasi-monopoly". The Commission said the merger would have led to higher fares for four million of the six million Greek and European passengers flying to and from Athens each year. The European Commission also blocked the merger of Ryanair and Aer Lingus in 2007. Since then the major shareholders in Aer Lingus, Ryanair and the Irish government, have indicated that they may sell their stakes in the airline. This could leave International Airlines Group (British Airways/Iberia) bidding for Aer Lingus and its valuable landing slots at Heathrow Airport.

European cross-border mergers and acquisitions have soared in recent years as EU firms seek to compete in an increasingly competitive global market. As trade barriers come down in an enlarged EU, cross-border mergers have become more popular especially as the introduction of the euro has removed currency risks. Recent examples of cross-border mergers have been the acquisition of the Dutch airline KLM by Air France and that of Abbey National by the Spanish bank Santander.

The EU Commission will consider investigating any merger involving worldwide sales greater than €5bn or where EU sales of at least two of the companies exceed €250m. The Commission has the power to bar activities which contravene either **Article 81** or **82** and impose fines on companies it judges to have been

Air France was one of a number of airlines fined by the European Commission for fixing the price of air cargo.

at fault to a maximum of 10% of world wide turnover. Many of the changes in UK competition policy introduced by the 1998 Competition Act brought the UK broadly into line with EU competition law.

Where the effect of anti-competitive behaviour extends beyond the UK to other EU-member states, this is now prohibited by Articles 101 and 102 of the Treaty on the Functioning of the European Union (TFEU). This Treaty goes into deeper detail on the role, policies and operation of the EU with anti-competitive agreements (under the Chapter I and Article 101 prohibitions), and abuse of dominant market position (under the Chapter II/Article 102 prohibitions).

In 2006 a cartel involving synthetic rubber producers was punished by the Commission, although the 'whistle blower' Bayer was exempt from fines imposed on other cartel members. In 2008 four glass firms were fined a total of €1.38bn for fixing the price of glass used in the automotive industry. Vehicle manufacturers indicated that they might pursue the glass makers, which include the UK based firm Pilkington.

In late 2011 the European Commission fined 11 airlines almost 800m euros for fixing the price of air cargo between 1999 and 2006. EU Competition Commissioner Joaquin Almunia said: "it is deplorable that so many major airlines coordinated their pricing to the detriment of European businesses and European consumers." Air France-KLM were given the biggest fine but Luthansa escaped a fine because it had alerted the regulatory authorities to the existence of the cartel.

Airline	Fine (euros)
Air France-KLM (includes Martinair)	339.6m
British Airways	104m
Cargolux	79.9m
Singapore Airlines	74.8m
SAS	70.2m
Cathay Pacific	57.1m
Japan Airlines	35.7m
Air Canada	21.0m
Qantas	8.9m
LAN Chile	8.2m

Source: European Commission

The European Competition Commission is empowered by the amended **Treaty of Rome** to apply the above Articles and enjoys a number of investigative powers such as inspection of premises and written requests for information. Substantial fines are also at its disposal for violations. Since May 2004 all competition authorities in EU member states are empowered to apply fully the provisions of the Treaty in order to ensure that competition is not distorted or restricted. In order to strengthen the EU's fight against cartels and to speed up investigations a separate cartel directorate has been created within the Commission.

An important issue to consider when a firm or group of firms is being investigated for anti-competitive practices is whether firms should have to prove that they are innocent rather than the competition authorities have to prove their guilt as is the case now, i.e. if you think that you are not abusing your dominant position prove it!

Question 15.2

Unilever and Procter & Gamble fined for running a cartel

In 2011 the consumer products firms Unilever and Procter & Gamble were fined 315m euros for fixing washing powder prices in eight European countries. These fines follow an investigation by the European Competition Commission after a tip-off by the German company, Henkel which was part of the cartel but escaped a fine because of its co-operation with the authorities.

Investigate the background to this case.
http://www.bbc.co.uk/news/business-13064928

Question 15.3

Study Figure 15.1 below, which shows how an investigation of a monopoly with significant economies of scale can pose problems for competition authorities when the marginal and average costs of the monopolist (ACm/MCm) is below that of firms in a competitive market (MCc/ACc).

Figure 15.1

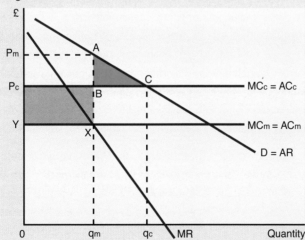

What is the significance of the two shaded areas for the competition authorities?

Unit 16: **Market failure**

The comparison of perfect competition and monopoly from the perspective of allocative efficiency (see Unit 12) yielded the conclusion that perfectly competitive markets, by equating the marginal cost of provision to the marginal benefit of consumption, maximise net social utility (benefit). This analysis gives powerful impetus to those who argue in favour of a competitive free market economy. However, left entirely to its own devices a free market economy will always fail to produce a socially optimal outcome. Market failure stems from the following sources:

1. The existence of monopoly power

A monopoly is allocatively and productively inefficient because price is above marginal cost and output is below minimum average cost. Monopoly results in a lower consumer surplus than in competitive markets and a deadweight welfare loss. These issues were discussed in Units 8 and 15.

2. Lack of provision of public goods

Public goods are defined by two characteristics. They are **non-excludable** in the sense that if the good is provided at all we cannot prevent anyone benefiting from the good or service in question. Further, public goods are **non-rivalrous** (non-diminishable) in consumption, so that one person's consumption of the good does not leave any less for anyone else to enjoy. Many public goods possess a third characteristic, **non-rejectability** meaning that it is not possible to choose not to consume the good or service. Thus national defence is a prime example of a pure public good. If the country is attacked we cannot single out one individual and refuse to protect him; similarly, one person's enjoyment of the benefits of the national defence system does not leave any less for another person to enjoy; and it would be very difficult for an individual to remain in the country and choose not to benefit. Public goods are to be contrasted with private goods, which are rivalrous, excludable and usually rejectable (consider a chocolate bar, for example). Many goods possess some, but not all, of the characteristics of public goods and are known as **quasi-public goods**. Television signals, for instance, are non-rivalrous and are non-excludable unless a system of signal scrambling and decoders is operated. On the other hand, the signals are certainly rejectable. Satellite TV is much closer to being a private good. Sea and flood defences are categorised as public goods. The market is unlikely to be interested in supplying public goods because of the free-rider principle. Hence the government provides them via the taxation system.

Quite obviously there is a collective need for public goods. The provision of defence, for example, is necessary for the security of a country and the stability of its economic system. Yet, this service cannot be marketed since anyone who does not pay for the service cannot be excluded from benefiting from it. It follows that if the service is to be provided, it must be done by government. This raises, of course, the issue of efficiency.

Since marginal cost represents the opportunity cost of providing a good or service, it follows that allocation is efficient if marginal cost equals price. If it were possible for the government to establish what each individual was prepared to pay for defence, and assuming that the supply was variable, then its supply could be expanded until the marginal cost of the last unit equalled the price which the community was collectively prepared to pay for it. This proposition can be illustrated by the diagram in Figure 16.1.

For simplicity's sake, we assume that the community consists of two individuals who place a different value on defence. Their demand curves are shown on the diagram as D_1 and D_2. From these curves it is possible to draw a third curve which expresses their joint demand, D3. The efficient allocation of the community's resources to defence is represented by quantity OQ, where the joint price which the two individuals are prepared to pay equals the marginal cost. The problem would be to get people to reveal what they would be willing to pay for a particular quantity of defence. It is in the interest of the individual to understate their true valuation and depend on other members of the community to provide the service. This is the **free-rider principle**.

Figure 16.1: Public goods

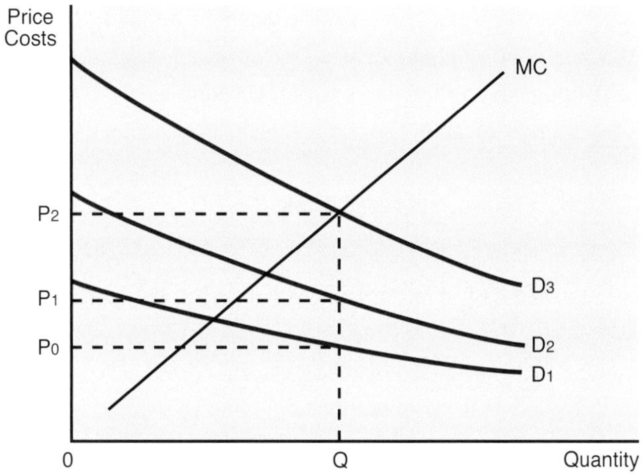

The joint price P_2 ($OP_0 + OP_1$) = MC. Thus the allocation of resources to defence would be allocatively efficient.

Because of the free-rider principle, the cost of public goods is met out of taxes. Those who value a particular good or service more than the average valuation gain more than those who value it as less than the average valuation, but it is hoped that these differences balance themselves out so that the provision of the service by the government is allocatively efficient.

The **marginal cost** of providing a public good to one extra person is zero. If the population of a country rises by one then the marginal cost of providing national defence to that person is zero. As the price of a public good at point of consumption is zero than price = marginal cost and thus government provision is allocatively efficient.

Thus the conventional policy solution is for the government to take responsibility for the provision of public goods, and to ensure that everyone contributes to the cost of provision through the collection of taxes. Where this is done, there is a high chance of productive inefficiency, given the lack of a profit incentive. It is for this reason that the government's privatisation programme has included the 'contracting out' of the provision of a number of public services to the private sector (see Unit 18). Roads have often be seen as a quasi-public good because some major roads and motorways could be operated via the private sector. This has happened with the M6 Toll road around Birmingham. Midland Expressway operates the M6 Toll and as can be seen from the data below also engages in **price discrimination** depending on the time of day the road is used.

M6 Toll Charges

Guide	Mon-Fri (06:00-23:00)	Sat-Sun (06:00-23:00)	Night (23:00-06:00)
Class 1 (e.g. motorbike)	£3.00	£2.80	£1.80
Class 2 (e.g. saloon car)	£5.50	£4.80	£3.80
Class 3 (e.g. saloon car & trailer)	£10.00	£8.60	£6.60
Class 4 (e.g. van/coach)	£11.00	£9.60	£8.60
Class 5 (e.g. HGV)	£11.00	£9.60	£8.60

Source: Midland Expressway Ltd

Midland Expressway designed, constructed, and now operates and maintains the M6 Toll road which will be handed back to the government in 2054.

Privately operated motorways could become the future as tolling is introduced extensively to relieve the congested motorway system. Tolling is likely to become easier in the years ahead with the use of satellite technology. Private sector involvement in what were traditionally public sector projects such as road building are popular with many politicians because there is so much pressure on government expenditure in other areas such as health and education.

Road pricing has its attractions with road congestion worsening on major UK roads. Building more motorways is not a long term option as supply tends to create its own demand. However, the UK has fewer miles of motorway per head of population than many other EU countries and the widening of motorways such as the M4 and M6 is likely to go ahead in the coming years, possibly by using the hard shoulders as extra lanes. New satellite technology and the ability to price discriminate will make road pricing inevitable though despite the fact that road tolls are a **regressive tax**.

In recent years there has been increasing criticism of the high cost of motoring in the UK compared to other EU countries. However, the real cost of motoring has fallen in the UK mainly due to falling car prices. Petrol prices remain high with Excise Duty and VAT accounting for over 65% of the price of a litre of petrol. In mainland Europe motoring costs are increased by road tolls, and if tolls were extensively established on major motorways in the UK it is likely that tax on petrol would fall. This would particularly benefit drivers in rural areas who do not contribute significantly to congestion but currently pay high road taxes.

In March 2012 the coalition government announced a feasibility study to work out ways in which private firms could be brought in to run motorways and major trunk roads on long-term leases. According to the briefing, in exchange these firms might receive a proportion of the vehicle excise duty or be able to receive revenue from **shadow tolls**. The firms would be paid by the government for the number of vehicles which used the road. If these firms substantially increased road capacity, for example by adding new lanes or building new motorways, they could charge tolls. The government has stressed that this is not privatisation because the state would remain the ultimate owner of the road. Clearly the government's priority is to improve the UK's infrastructure but the huge fiscal deficit makes large scale public sector funding very difficult. Private sector involvement in public sector activities is covered in more detail in Unit 18.

3. Merit and demerit goods

Merit goods are those that would be under-provided in a pure, free market economy; conversely, demerit goods are those which would be over-provided. In practice, it is a value judgement as to what is or is not a merit or demerit good, creating a need for government intervention. From a theoretical point of view however, under- or over-provision by the market would occur wherever there is a divergence between private and social costs and benefits, through the existence of externalities. An **externality** is a cost or benefit accruing to a third party as a result of another agent's activity. Thus, the passer-by who enjoys the beautiful garden planted by the occupier benefits from a positive externality, while the neighbour troubled by loud music from next door suffers from a negative externality. Even in the absence of externalities, under- or over-provision could result from a failure on the part of economic agents to measure accurately the extent of private costs or benefits. External costs and benefits are not reflected in the market price of a product.

Part of the case for the free or subsidised provision of merit goods by the government depends on the divergence of private and social costs and benefits. State education is a merit good which is provided free at the point of consumption. However, unlike most private goods, it provides a **positive externality** (external benefit). Education obviously benefits the child and its family. A well-educated population brings benefits to the whole community in terms of greater productivity. Theoretically, the optimum allocation of resources to education would be where government expenditure was matched by the positive externality.

The provision of merit goods by the government can also be justified in terms of **equity**. The free market efficiently allocates scarce resources by meeting the demand for goods and services at a price. People who cannot afford to purchase those goods or services do not benefit from them. Education is considered to be individually and socially valuable and therefore, on the grounds of equity or fairness, it is argued that income should be redistributed through taxation to provide a universal service.

In the analysis of Unit 4, it was implicitly assumed that private costs and benefits were equal to social costs and benefits leading to the conclusion that the socially optimal level of output for a market is reached where marginal (private) benefit and marginal (private) cost are equated. We are now in a position to appreciate that the existence of externalities means that the optimal resource allocation occurs where marginal social benefit is equal to marginal social cost. It should be noted that:

Marginal social benefit (MSB) = marginal private benefit (MPB) + marginal external benefit (MEB)

and

Marginal social cost (MSC) = marginal private cost (MPC) + marginal external cost (MEC).

The existence of external benefits when merit goods such as health are consumed means that in a free market the good is under-consumed. In the diagram below (Figure 16.2) the government could increase output to the socially efficient level by a per unit subsidy increasing supply to S_1. The subsidy would lower the price and increase output to Q_1.

Figure 16.2: Merit goods

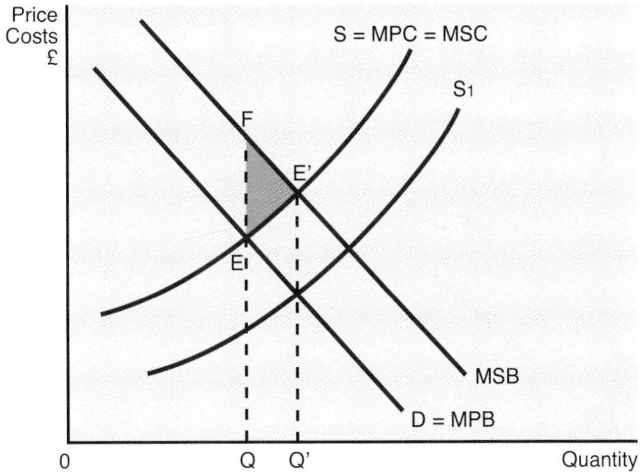

Given that MPC and MSC coincide because there are no external costs, and that MSB exceeds D (MPB) because of external benefits, the socially efficient outcome is at E', where MSB = MSC. However, the free market equilibrium where D = MPC is at E and thus output is too low at Q for social efficiency. Welfare loss is given by the shaded area EFE' but the subsidy will eliminate this raising quantity to Q'. Demerit goods such as alcohol and tobacco have negative consumption externalities based on the limited information of drinkers and smokers. The socially optimal level of consumption in Figure 16.3 is Q_3 which is at a level that takes into account the information failure of consumers and the external costs.

Consumption of demerit goods often leads to **retrospective regret** – a term used to describe people who in later life regret consumption of cigarettes or alcohol in their younger years. This is a very good reason for high taxes and negative advertising of these types of goods because in the early years of high alcohol or tobacco consumption there appear to be no long run side effects. There is thus an **information gap** for these consumers.

Figure 16.3

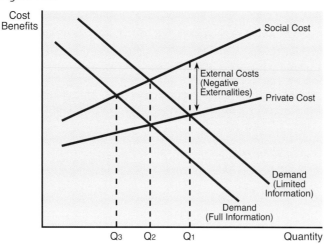

4. External costs

An external cost from production such as pollution may cause marginal social cost to diverge from marginal private cost. In Figure 16.4 the demand curve reflects the marginal social benefit (MSB) because there are no external benefits. As there are external costs the marginal social cost (MSC) is greater than the marginal private cost (MPC).

The social efficient outcome is at Q_1 (MSB = MSC), but the free market outcome is at Q. Output is too high and price too low for social efficiency. The welfare loss is the shaded area EE'F. The consumption of **demerit goods** such as cigarettes produces the same effects.

Figure 16.4

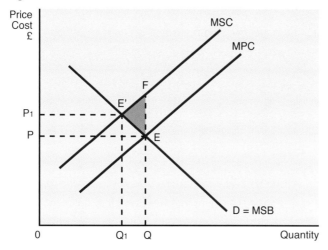

Available policy options include the following:

1. **Impose a specific unit tax**, equal to the marginal external cost (shown as EF on the diagram), on the suppliers of goods creating negative externalities (external costs). This serves to shift the supply curve (MPC) so that it lies on top of the marginal social cost curve. The **Climate Change Levy** was introduced in 2001 and is an environmental tax on energy supplies to industry, commerce, agriculture, local administration and a number of other services. The Climate Change Levy is intended to encourage greater energy efficiency and lower energy use by increasing the effective price of energy by between 10% and 15%. As such, it aims to help the UK to meet its legally binding commitments under the Kyoto Protocol to reduce greenhouse gas emissions. The main problem with taxes of this kind is that it is very hard to value the external costs in order to place a value on the tax of the product.

The Australian government has decided that from July 2012 it will impose a **carbon tax** on carbon emissions for its worst polluting firms which include coal fired electricity generators and steel manufacturers. Carbon dioxide emissions would be taxed at A\$23 (\$25; £15) per tonne. Australia has the highest CO_2 emissions per head in the developed world and it is hoped that the carbon tax will reduce emissions of carbon by 160 million tonnes over the next ten years.

2. **Legislate** to place an upper limit on the level of negative externalities an economic agent is allowed to generate. Car and aircraft emissions could be targets for such legislation. This would then impose costs on manufacturers to produce cleaner engines.

3. **Extending property rights.** Any negative externalities are generated because of the incomplete allocation of property rights, sometimes called the **Tragedy of the Commons**. No-one owns the rights to the air that surrounds us for example, so no-one is in a position to say that their property right has been violated when a factory pollutes the atmosphere. Equally the absence of property rights in fishing areas has led to over-fishing with disastrous consequences for areas such as the Grand Banks of Newfoundland and also the North Sea. **Coase's theorem** states that as long as there is complete allocation of property rights markets can provide a socially optimal solution to the problem of externalities. Consider, for example, the fish farm that operates down-stream from a chemical factory that pollutes the water. If no-one owns the right to the water, there is a problem. If, however, the government were to give tradeable **pollution permits** to the chemical company, effectively granting it property rights, the problem can be overcome. The fishery is now in a position to offer to buy some or all of the permits from the chemical company. Trade in permits will take place while both parties benefit from the exchange. When a point is reached where no further mutually beneficial trade of permits is possible, no further trade will take place and a socially optimal solution is secured. It would have made no difference had the permits been allocated to the fish farm; the chemical company would then have purchased permits to a sufficient extent to secure the best outcome. This policy is known as 'internalising the externality' because it brings it within the market framework.

It should be noted that the first two policy options face the difficulty of identifying the socially optimal level of output and consumption and deciding the extent of intervention required to bring that level of consumption about. Valuing the external costs is always a difficulty.

5. Asymmetry of information

Asymmetry of information occurs when one party to a transaction has more or better information than the other party. In most cases it is the seller that knows more about the product than the buyer, however, it is possible for the reverse to be true — for the buyer to know more than the seller. Examples of situations where the seller usually has better information than the buyer are numerous and include used-car sellers, stockbrokers, estate agents, and sellers of life insurance and pensions.

Royal & Sun Alliance, one of the UK's largest insurance groups, was fined £1.35m in 2002 for failing to provide compensation to over 13,000 of its customers who were mis-sold pensions. The Financial Services Authority (FSA), said it had fined life insurance companies within the Royal & Sun Alliance group as a result of "systematic weaknesses" in the pensions review they carried out in the period to August 2000.

The pensions review was set up by the Personal Investment Authority, a predecessor to the FSA. Firms at the time were obliged to contact customers who took out personal pensions with them between June 1994 and April 1998, a period when a number of pensions were found to have been mis-sold. Mis-selling occurred when people were sold personal pensions by commission-hungry salesmen when they would have been better off staying in, or joining, their employer's scheme.

Equitable Life almost collapsed in 2000 and had to cut the pensions and retirement savings of its policy-holders to remain afloat, causing a major public outcry. Many would argue that the company promised returns that were unrealistic to potential customers who had insufficient information to make an informed

choice. In July 2008 the Parliamentary Ombudsman's report recommended that the government issue an apology for its poor regulation and that a compensation scheme be set up for investors who had lost money.

In his 1970 work *The Market for Lemons* George Akerlof used the term asymmetric information. He noticed that, in a **'lemon' market**, the average value of a product tends to go down, even for those products of perfectly good quality. The second-hand car market is a good example of this where there are good used cars and defective used cars (called the lemons). The buyer of a car does not know before buying whether a car is a good car or a 'lemon.' Thus the buyer's best guess for a given car is that the car is of average quality, as a result only an average price will be offered by the potential buyer. This will make the owners of good second hand cars unwilling to place their cars on the second-hand car market because they will not get a decent enough price to make it worthwhile for them. If this process continues the quality of cars on the market will keep on declining with the bad cars driving out the good ones. **(Gresham's Law)**. Eventually the market may disappear altogether.

Asymmetry of information can lead to a misallocation of resources and a welfare loss because goods and services will not be allocated to those who want them most, but those who have the most money.

In 2012 many people in the UK received compensation for the mis-selling of personal protection insurance (PPI). This type of insurance covers borrowers if they are unable to make their repayments on loans or credit cards due to illness or loss of employment. The regulator, the Financial Services Authority (FSA), ordered the major banks who sold PPI to pay compensation to borrowers because of mis-selling – usually because it was not explained properly with some people taking it out who did not need it or not being entitled to it if they actually did make a claim.

It can also be the case that the buyer may know more about a product than the seller. The owner of a junk shop, with no knowledge of antique furniture, might price an old chest of drawers at £50. An antiques expert might come into the shop and realise that the drawers are worth £5,000 but pay only the marked price, taking advantage of the seller's lack of knowledge.

Landfill tax

Landfill tax is paid on top of normal landfill fees by businesses and local authorities that want to dispose of waste using a landfill site. It is designed to encourage businesses to produce less waste and to use alternative forms of waste management such as recycling. There are two rates of tax – £2.50 per tonne for inactive waste such as rocks and soil and the standard rate – £64 per tonne for all other land filled waste. The rate will increase to £72 per tonne on 1 April 2013 and £80 per tonne on 1 April 2014. The government plans that by 2013, the waste sent to landfills should be 50% of that sent in 1995.

The UK has had a very poor record on recycling and is running out of landfill sites which themselves can become unstable and a threat to the environment. The Landfill tax should encourage the local authorities to instigate schemes whereby householders separate products such as glass, cardboard, paper and plastics from the rest of the household refuse. However, if taxes are too high on the disposal of waste in landfill sites it will encourage illegal fly-tipping. In a bid to catch up with many countries in Europe the government has targeted that 33% of household waste should be recycled or composted by 2015.

The Kyoto Treaty and beyond

The Kyoto Protocol is an international agreement setting targets for industrialised countries to cut greenhouse gas emissions which are seen as responsible for global warming. Industrialised countries have committed to cut their combined emissions by 5% below 1990 levels between 2008 and 2012. The Kyoto Protocol became a legally binding treaty in February 2005. All of the major industrialised nations have signed the Protocol except the United States, whose greenhouse gas emissions are the largest for any single country. Russia signed Kyoto belatedly in September 2004 but rapidly industrialising countries such as China and India are not covered under the Protocol, neither are developing countries in general. By

2025 China will overtake the United States as the top emitter of the greenhouse gases causing global warming, although the United States will still have the highest emissions per head of population.

Under the Kyoto Protocol the UK has a legally binding target to reduce emissions of greenhouse gases by 12.5% relative to 1990 levels between 2008 and 2012. The Kyoto Protocol allows for 'flexible mechanisms', such as emissions trading, and the clean development mechanism (CDM) for countries to achieve their targets. Most environmentalists believe that the Kyoto Protocol is only a minor step forward in the battle against global warming and warn of a 'tipping point' when global warming will be irreversible. Kyoto will not prevent the 'tipping point' being reached according to some scientists, who warn that more radical measures are now needed to reduce emissions.

The United Nations Climate Change Conference was held in Durban, South Africa, in late 2011 to establish a new treaty to limit carbon emissions once Kyoto expires. The conference agreed to a legally binding deal comprising all countries, which will be prepared by 2015, and take effect in 2020. There was also progress regarding the creation of a Climate Change Fund which will distribute $100 billion per year to help poor countries adapt to the impact of climate change. The European Union agreed to place its current emissions targets inside the legally binding Kyoto Protocol, a key demand of developing countries. Although the conference was declared a success, scientists and environmental groups warned that the deal was not sufficient to avoid global warming beyond the 2°C 'tipping point' and that more urgent action was needed.

The European Union Emissions Trading Scheme

The EU **Emissions Trading Scheme** is one of the main policies being introduced across Europe to tackle emissions of carbon dioxide and other greenhouse gases to combat the serious threat of climate change.

The Scheme started in 2005, establishing the world's largest market in greenhouse gas emissions. The first phase of the scheme ran from 1st January 2005 to 31 December 2007, with a second phase from 1st January 2008 to 31st December 2012. The second phase coincides with the first Kyoto Commitment Period. The scheme operates on a 'cap and trade' basis. EU member state governments are required to set an emissions cap for each of the installations covered by the scheme. Each installation is allocated allowances (permits) for the particular commitment period in question. The number of allowances allocated to each installation for any given period is set down in a document called the National Allocation Plan and each member state has such a Plan. Installations covered by the Scheme are in the energy and mineral industries, pulp and paper production and iron and steel making.

Each installation involved in the Scheme must carefully monitor its emissions every year. It will then need to surrender a number of EU emission allowances equal to the number of tonnes of carbon dioxide emitted for that year. These surrendered allowances will then be cancelled. Therefore the installation has to ensure that there are sufficient allowances in its account to cover the emissions for that year.

There are three routes an installation can employ to ensure that the allowances it holds match its emissions:

1. Reduce the installation's own annual emissions to the number of allowances allocated for that year;

2. Reduce annual emissions to below the cap and either sell the excess allowances to another company or 'bank' them for future use;

3. If the annual emissions are above the allowances allocated, the company owning the installation may buy allowances from the market to cover the difference. The price in the market will depend on the supply of, and demand for, carbon allowances within the Europe wide carbon trading market. Markets in these EU pollution permits are already in operation, but there has been some criticism that member states have been rather generous in the allocation of permits not putting enough pressure on installations to reduce their emissions. The European Commission, meanwhile, has produced the ambitious '20/20/20 by 2020' plan: emissions cuts of 20% over 1990 levels allied to a 20% gain in energy efficiency and 20% of energy from renewables by 2020.

Figure 16.5: CO₂ emission allowances

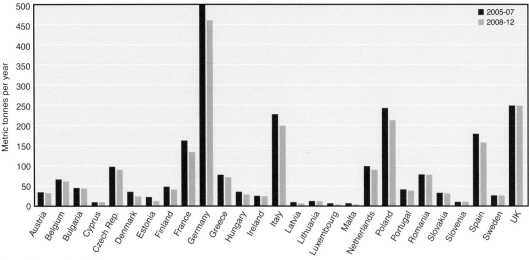

Source: European Commission

The biggest growth area for greenhouse gas emissions is in air transport and airlines have joined the EU Emissions Trading Scheme. However this produced strong objections by China and the US although legal challenges to the ETS by American Airlines and other US carriers have now been dropped. British Airways favour a permit scheme to a fuel tax which has been seen as another option for reducing aircraft emissions. At present jet fuel is largely untaxed and airlines and their customers are paying little towards the external costs of air travel except the **Air Passenger Duty**. Airlines are opposed to a fuel tax partly because fixing the right level of tax to achieve an environmental objective is unclear. In any case there would have to be some international agreement on the level of tax to make it effective. British Airways feel that the pollution permit scheme is superior because a clear emissions limit is set. In addition the airline feel that if permits are allocated free to polluters those firms that achieve the biggest reductions in emissions can gain financially by selling their permits on the carbon trading market.

In January 2008, the European Commission proposed a number of changes to the Emissions Trading Scheme (ETS), including centralised allocation of permits by an EU authority and the auctioning of a greater share (60+ %) of permits rather than allocating them freely, as well as the inclusion of other greenhouse gases in the scheme. These changes are only likely to become effective from January 2013 onwards, i.e. in the 3rd Trading Period under the EU ETS. Also, the proposed caps for the 3rd Trading Period foresee an overall reduction of greenhouse gases for the sector of 21% in 2020 compared to 2005 emissions. Phase III of the EU ETS will run from 1 January 2013 to 31 December 2020.

The theory of second best

Intuition tells us that if market failure exists, that is, it is not the case (even in the absence of externalities) that MPB (= P) = MC in all markets, then it is surely best to ensure that P = MC in as many as possible. According to the theory of Lipsey and Lancaster, this is not so. Suppose that P > MC in one market but P = MC in all others. This would encourage too much consumption of all other goods relative to the highly priced one. It would be more efficient to have P > MC in all markets, allowing consumption patterns to be the same as if P = MC in all markets. The economist A.C. Pigou encapsulates this idea by employing an analogy with a tight-rope walker. If he has a suitcase in his left hand (an impediment to efficient performance) it is better to place a suitcase in his right hand (restoring balance) rather than to try to take the first suitcase away (lest its sudden removal should cause him to topple over).

The theory of second best has important implications for policy making. It is possible that a constant drive to increase competition is not the best policy, given that it is never possible to ensure perfect competition in all markets. If the first-best solution were achieved in one market by government intervention so that

MSB = MSC it may then aggravate problems elsewhere. A second-best solution needs to be adopted as a compromise.

Cost benefit analysis

Cost benefit analysis is a technique of investment appraisal which is often used in large scale construction projects which involve public/state spending and potentially could have a significant impact on the wider society. While private sector investment projects are only analysed for their private costs and benefits over their lifetime, cost benefit studies additionally include the impact of external costs and benefits when assessing a project's viability. With taxpayers money involved in many cases the project's impact on society is a key part of cost benefit analysis.

Social benefits = Private benefits + external benefits and Social costs = Private costs + external costs. A cost benefit study will attempt to calculate the net social benefit which is Social costs – Social benefit. In theory a project will go ahead if the net social benefit is positive. In carrying out a cost benefit study all the costs and benefits (private and external) will have been given a monetary value and the study will have had to take into account the lifetime of the project which could possibly be over 50 years. In recent years cost benefit studies are relevant to projects such as Crossrail (the east-west London train route), a third runway at Heathrow, the Severn barrage (to generate tidal power from the River Severn estuary) and HS2, the high speed London to Birmingham rail link.

However, cost benefit analysis does pose several problems. It is a matter of opinion as to which external costs and benefits should be included and which excluded. In addition placing a monetary value on externalities is difficult and complex with a system called '**shadow pricing**' often being used. Projects subject to cost benefit analysis are often projected to last for many years – maybe 50 or more. Even when values are calculated for externalities they need to be projected forward (which is difficult in itself) and then they need to be discounted to present day values using a percentage discount factor. Hence setting the framework for a cost benefit study is not only complex but arguably it can be drawn up so as to produce the findings that are wanted by supporters of the project (maybe the government or other vested interests such as construction firms). The terms of reference for a cost benefit study for the proposed HS2 rail project would be drawn up differently by Greenpeace or Friends of the Earth when compared to those used by the Department of Transport. Cost benefit analysis is also a very time consuming and expensive procedure.

Question 16.1

(a) What private costs are associated with car ownership?

(b) What external costs does use of the private car impose? What about external benefits?

(c) Is it possible to put a monetary value on externalities?

(d) Discuss the relative merits of the following policies designed to alleviate the problem of increased use of the private car?
  (i)   Heavy state subsidising of public transport.
  (ii) Increase road tax (a lump sum annual payment made by car users).
  (iii) Increase fuel tax.
  (iv) Introduce tolls, with a higher price being charged at peak traffic periods (note that road space is currently allocated by queuing).
  (v)   Changes in planning laws.

(e) Classify the motor car as an economic good (public or private; luxury or necessity; merit or demerit).

Question 16.2

Follow the links below to examine recent developments in the European Emissions Trading Scheme.

http://www.bbc.co.uk/news/world-europe-17351137

http://news.bbc.co.uk/today/hi/today/newsid_8503000/8503506.stm

http://ec.europa.eu/clima/policies/ets/index_en.htm

Question 16.3

In the context of road building to ease congestion explain the statement, "supply creates its own demand".

Question 16.4

Explain why the use of pollution permits could lead to pollution becoming heavily localised.

Question 16.5

"Carbon floor price" plans dealt a blow by MPs

by Fiona Harvey, environment correspondent, *The Guardian*, 26 January 2012.

Plans to prop up the price of carbon for businesses would push up the cost of energy and disadvantage British companies, say select committee.

Government plans to prop up the price of emitting carbon dioxide for businesses have been dealt a blow by MPs, who have blasted the proposals as a handicap to British companies.

The 'carbon floor price' would ensure that companies were paying a minimum price for producing carbon, in contrast to the **European Union**'s existing **emissions trading** scheme under which the price of emissions can plunge to near zero. By propping up the cost of carbon, and therefore of fossil fuel energy, the floor price is intended to encourage companies to use energy more efficiently, thereby saving money, and install new technology to cut carbon.

But the influential energy and **climate change** select committee of MPs said in a report published on Thursday that a floor price would push up the cost of energy and disadvantage British companies relative to their European and international rivals, which will not be subject to a minimum price for carbon.

The floor price was a key plank in the Tory party's green policies, as part of its pre-election manifesto. However, the idea has been attacked by business groups and the chancellor, George Osborne, has appeared markedly cooler on green policies in recent months.

Tim Yeo, chairman of the committee, said: "The chancellor was right to say we won't save the planet by putting the UK out of business. Ironically, however, it is the Treasury's decision to set a carbon price floor that could result in industry and electricity production relocating to other EU countries."

Current EU carbon prices are languishing at little above €7 per tonne of carbon emitted, a long way below the price of €25 to €40 that analysts say is necessary to have an influence on business decisions. The government's proposed price floor of about £16 a tonne would provide a stronger signal to companies to encourage investment in low-carbon technologies and business processes, and would provide cash to the Treasury, which would receive the extra revenues from the price floor.

But Yeo said that by going it alone with a price floor, the UK would be creating a disadvantage for industry, relative to **Europe** and the rest of the world, and criticised plans that would ensure the money raised from the floor price flowed to the Treasury. "Unless the price of carbon is increased at an EU-wide level, taking action on our own will have no overall effect on emissions other than to out-source them," he said. "A revenue raising exercise disguised as a green policy won't help anybody, the price of carbon has to be increased at an EU level to kick start investment in clean-energy."

The Treasury said: "The chancellor has made clear that the UK should go no slower but also no faster than other European countries in cutting emissions. To do this we need to reduce our emissions in the way that works best for circumstances in this country. The carbon price floor is vital in reducing uncertainty and creating incentives for investment in low carbon electricity generation now so we have lower emissions in the future."

An official pointed out that last year, in the chancellor's autumn statement, the government announced £250m of support for businesses affected by its green policies, including £100m in compensation for the added indirect costs of the carbon price floor.

Chris Hewett of Green Alliance said the sums imposed by the proposed floor price were not high enough to influence business decisions to the degree needed to change behaviour. "The carbon price floor is a small step in the right direction, but it is not a dramatic increase [in the price of carbon]. It is there to provide a modest boost to the price of carbon under the EU emissions trading scheme – but it's only a marginal increase and it is certainly not going to cripple anyone."

But some green campaigners agreed with the committee that the government should reconsider its plans. Joss Garman, campaigner at Greenpeace, said: "George Osborne's proposed carbon floor price will be ineffective, adding to the squeeze on families and business while making negligible cuts in pollution. The truth is that the only real beneficiary of this plan is the chancellor's balance sheet." He added: "This is precisely the sort of measure that destroys public confidence in environmental policies."

Damien Morris, of the Sandbag campaigning group, said: "We agree with the committee's findings that the UK carbon floor price imposes unnecessary costs on British businesses and consumers. The government would be far better focusing on ways to reduce the volume of emissions allowances currently in circulation. In this context, it is imperative that all British MEPs support key proposals to reform the emissions trading scheme as they are voted on in Brussels over the coming weeks."

Some business analysts also backed up the select committee's views and called for changes to the EU emissions trading scheme as a whole, instead of unilateral action by the UK. Jonathan Grant, carbon markets specialist at the consultancy PwC, said: "The UK carbon price floor is one of the best examples of carbon leakage – a policy that doesn't reduce emissions but simply shifts them from one country to another. As all power companies in Europe are covered by an EU-wide cap, unilateral measures in the UK won't reduce emissions overall."

Instead, he said, a carbon price floor in the UK would merely work to subsidise coal-fired power generation in the rest of Europe, as a lower demand for carbon permits in the UK would mean more were available for companies on the continent, pushing down the prices for high-emitting power plants there.

Grant said: "An EU-wide carbon floor price would be more effective in stimulating low-carbon investment and reduce the risk of outsourcing carbon to another country."

Reproduced by the kind permission of *The Guardian*.

Question: Investigate the case for and against a floor price (minimum price) for pollution permits in the European Union.

Unit 17: **The market for corporate control**

The role of shareholders as a discipline on the firm

Shareholders, as the owners of a firm, are risk-takers (i.e. they play part of the role of the entrepreneur – see Unit 1). Having invested in a company by buying its shares, they are entitled to a share of its profits (known as dividends). A second potential source of return on the investment comes in the form of a capital gain. If the company performs well, the price of its shares is likely to increase, allowing shareholders to sell their shares at a profit. However, if the company makes a loss no dividend has to be paid. In the event of the company going bankrupt, shareholders may lose the money they have invested altogether.

As a rule of thumb, there is a correspondence between the level of risk entailed in an investment and its potential return. This provides the basis for the distinction between two types of shareholder. **Preference shareholders** receive a fixed dividend and, if profits are small, are entitled to receive that dividend before any payment is made to ordinary shareholders. Although neither type of shareholder will necessarily receive a dividend if the company makes a loss, preference shareholders will be the first shareholders to get their money back if it goes bankrupt. It is thus clear that the ordinary shareholder faces the greater risk, but if profits are high they will receive a bigger dividend than the preference shareholder.

In theory, a firm will serve the interests of its owners. It is argued that shareholders act as a discipline on the firm because those who run it on a day to day basis, the managers and directors, are ultimately accountable to them (through Annual General Meetings, for example). Accordingly the company will seek to maximise profits and will not be able to be grossly inefficient, because costs must be minimised to this end.

There is not unanimous agreement that this account of the role of shareholders reflects reality. Unit 6 summarises alternative lines of analysis based around the divorce of ownership and control that might result from shareholders not being involved directly with the running of the company.

Even if one accepts that firms act to maximise profits some would argue that the influence of shareholders is not necessarily beneficial from an economic point of view. If shareholders require a rapid return on their investment, this is likely to lead the company to take a short term view of profit maximisation. 'Short termism' may result in companies rejecting investment projects that would deliver a high return in the long run, because the initial expense would entail smaller dividends today. Whether the projects foregone are investment in physical capital or human capital, the effect on the economy is detrimental.

In theory the competition for corporate control of **Public Limited Companies (PLC)** will ensure that long run **shareholder value** is maximised. If profits and dividends fall the market value of the firm's shares will also fall making it easier for the firm to be taken over by a hostile bidder who would quite possibly replace the old management with a new team who would reverse the decline. **The Takeover Panel** (Unit 15) looks into pending takeovers from the point of view of shareholder interests while the **Competition Commission** (Unit 15) uses a wider public interest criterion for its investigations.

An interesting battle for corporate control in 2004/05 was that concerning Manchester United PLC. The Glazier Family borrowed heavily to finance the purchase of the bulk of the firm's shares and then de-listed the company from the Stock Exchange reverting it to private ownership. The Glazier's felt that they could develop Manchester United's commercial potential better than the existing management. Many Manchester United supporters who also held small shareholdings in the club objected to the takeover using the slogan; "Man United is not for sale". However, Manchester United, by becoming a PLC years ago, was exactly that, for sale on a second hand share market.

Sometimes a bid for a PLC is not welcomed by its board of directors and this is called a **hostile bid**. In November 2009 UK confectioner Cadbury rejected a £9.8bn ($16.4bn) hostile bid from US food giant Kraft Foods. The Cadbury board said it "emphatically rejected" the offer, which nevertheless had to be put to its shareholders. Kraft offered a mixture of cash and shares for each Cadbury share. "Kraft's offer does not come remotely close to reflecting the true value of our company, and involves the unattractive prospect of the absorption of Cadbury into a low growth conglomerate business model," said the then Cadbury chairman Roger Carr.

However, by February 2010 the three men at the top of Cadbury announced their resignations following Kraft Foods' successful takeover of the chocolate maker. Chairman Roger Carr, chief executive Todd Stitzer and chief financial officer Andrew Bonfield all left. Kraft sealed its takeover after Cadbury shareholders voted in favour of the deal. Despite the Cadbury board's initial rejection of the hostile bid from Kraft it approved an increased bid of £11.5bn ($18.9bn) and advised shareholders to accept it, saying it offered substantial value for Cadbury shareholders. For many people this takeover was another example of a well established British company falling too easily into the hands of a foreign firm. When a hostile bid is launched the board of the takeover target might welcome a '**white knight**'. A white knight is a firm that makes a friendly takeover bid for a target company that is facing a hostile takeover.

Some firms prefer to remain **private limited companies** rather than have a full listing on the Stock Exchange by becoming a PLC. They prefer to keep a narrower share ownership so that shareholders cannot in their desire for short term returns, disrupt the long term investment plans of a company. Indeed Richard Branson's Virgin group returned to private ownership from PLC status partly for this reason. Many PLC's find that a large number of their shares are owned by institutional investors such as pension funds and insurance companies. These institutions can exert huge influence over the board of a PLC and arguably can exercise too much control over a company. The trend towards private ownership among large firms is quite noticeable and the number of firms with a full listing on the Stock Exchange fell for a time in recent years. Many City analysts blamed this on the complex corporate governance rules which apply to PLC's but not **private limited companies**. However, a listing on the London Stock Exchange is more attractive than a New York listing because of the financial and administrative burden of corporate governance regulations in the United States. However, it is worth noting that the number of listed companies in both the US and the UK has fallen dramatically since 1997, by 38% in the US and 48% in the UK.

It is interesting to note that corporate governance can take other forms. For example Network Rail (formerly Railtrack PLC) is a company **limited by guarantee**. This means that they are a private sector organisation and operate as a commercial business but they have no shareholders. Instead Network Rail is accountable to members, who do not receive dividends or share capital. All of Network's Rail's profits are reinvested into maintaining and upgrading the rail infrastructure. The board of directors of Network Rail is accountable to the members who include passenger groups and trade unions.

Royal Mail Group became a public limited company (plc) in 2001 but it remained wholly owned by the government. This created a more commercially focused company with greater freedom to borrow. At the same time a new regulatory regime was established with an independent regulator, Postcomm, and a reformed consumer body, Postwatch. At the time this gave the company commercial freedom without full privatisation, which many felt was necessary but politically sensitive.

Although its parcels business (Parcelforce) is doing well, mainly because of the growth of online shopping, Royal Mail has seen postal volumes fall by 25% since 2006 as a result of email and text messaging. These volumes are expected to continue to fall 25-40% in the next five years. In 2012 the postal service's new regulator Ofcom, allowed the price of first and second class stamps to rise to 50p and 60p respectively with Ofcom saying that the changes were needed to preserve the future of the universal postal service. Consumer Focus, which replaced Postwatch in speaking for postal consumers, felt that these price rises would lead to further decline in the use of the mail.

With further competitive pressure from private sector firms such as TNT and UK Mail the coalition government decided to take a radical step in the privatisation of the Royal Mail. The Postal Services Act

2011 allowed for up to 90% of the business to be sold, with a 10% stake for employees. Thus would be by a share sale and take place in 2014. In order to make the company more attractive to investors the assets and liabilities of the Royal Mail pension scheme are to be taken over by the government. Post Office Ltd (formerly Post Office Counters) provides a wide range of products such as stamps and banking through its network of post office branches. The company was previously a subsidiary of Royal Mail, but is now owned directly by the government and is not part of the planned privatisation.

Royal Mail is on track for privatisation.

The credit crunch and subsequent banking crisis in 2008/09 led to increased government holdings in commercial banks such as Lloyds/HBOS and the Royal Bank of Scotland (RBS). With many financial institutions on the brink of collapse the UK government bought sizeable stakes in banks with Northern Rock completely **nationalised**. The UK Government (HM Treasury) still holds an 84% stake in RBS. This stake, as with other government shareholdings in UK banks following the financial crisis, is held and managed through UK Financial Investments Limited, where voting rights as a shareholder are limited to 75% in order for the bank to retain its listing on the London Stock Exchange. In late 2011 it was announced that Virgin Money were going to buy Northern Rock for £747 million, from UK Financial Investments Limited. Although such moves by the government were seen as temporary in response to the crisis it is likely that the state will use its influence to change the way banks are run, in particular how exposed they are to risk and the size of bonuses paid to senior staff. It is also likely that the banking sector will become more tightly regulated both in the UK and globally.

Indeed the government is now engaging in legislative reform which will mean that the Financial Services Authority, the present regulator will no longer exist in its current form. The coalition government believes that at present, no single institution has the responsibility, authority and powers to monitor the financial system as a whole, and take appropriate action. Under the new legislation that power will now be given to the Bank of England. A new Prudential Regulation Authority (PRA) will be responsible for the day-to-day supervision of financial institutions that manage significant risk investments on their balance sheet. In addition the Financial Conduct Authority (FCA) will regulate how firms conduct their business. It will help to promote confidence and transparency in financial services and to give greater protection for consumers of financial services. It will also be empowered to promote competition in the financial sector.

In addition to reform of the regulatory regime, The Independent Commission on Banking headed by Sir John Vickers issued its report in 2011 which recommended that commercial banks should ring fence their high street retail banking from their high risk investment banking arms. Britain's banks are to be given until 2019 to implement radical reform of their operations to prevent another government rescue of the system. Sir John Vickers said that the reforms would cost between £4bn and £7bn but were more practical and less expensive than the full-scale separation of banks. However, with the enforced mergers of banks during the credit crunch the sector remains highly concentrated and in need of greater competition. Increased competition may possibly come from Tesco and Virgin in the coming years. The government will legislate to implement these proposed banking reforms before 2015.

The role of the Stock Exchange

The Stock Exchange provides a market mechanism for the exchange of second hand shares. Far fewer people would buy new shares in a company if there were no market to sell them on if they needed to sell at short notice. This is very important given the importance of new share issues for companies needing finance for new investment.

The existence of this mechanism provides a second discipline on the firm: the threat of hostile takeover bids. An inefficient company is likely to be subject to takeover attempts, because the inefficiency leads to it under-performing in terms of profits and this is likely to be reflected in its share price. This low share price makes the company an attractive proposition for predators who believe they can run the company more efficiently. Equally if a firm has a high price earnings ratio (P/E ratio) it may be attractive to buyers because its high current share price relative to low past earnings indicates promising future prospects.

It was argued above that the influence of shareholders might in fact damage the long run interests of the firm and the wider economy. Parallel arguments can be constructed with regard to the Stock Exchange and the threat of takeover. These may contribute to short termism as firms act to fend off hostile bids. In an attempt to do so, they may launch a drive for high short term profits, forsaking potentially profitable investment projects in the interests of paying higher dividends to keep the shareholders happy. This could lead to a loss of dynamic efficiency.

Further, some takeover bids are not based upon any perceived inefficiency in the company taken over. Horizontal integration (Unit 3), for example, results in greater market concentration and affords the newly combined firm greater control of its market. This might allow it to exploit consumers in the interests of increasing profit levels.

Question 17.1

(a) Explain the statement that "the shareholder plays part of the role of the entrepreneur".

(b) The exchange of shares is somewhat speculative in nature. One is likely to invest in a company if one expects its share price to rise, in the hope of making a capital gain. Explain the statement that "expectations of changes in share prices are self-fulfilling".

(c) Give three reasons why an individual might buy shares in a company quoted on the Stock Exchange.

Question 17.2

Private equity firms acquire control or a significant minority holding in a firm and then look to maximise the value of that investment. Boots the Chemist (Alliance Boots) was a public limited company (PLC) listed on the Stock Exchange but in 2007 it was bought out in a private equity transaction by KKR & Co. L.P.

Investigate the role of private equity groups in relation to the corporate control of UK firms.

Question 17.3

A sovereign wealth fund is a state-owned investment fund comprised of financial assets such as shares, government bonds, and property. 'Surplus' countries in the Middle and Far East are the most likely nations to be operating sovereign wealth funds.

Investigate the importance of sovereign wealth funds in the ownership of UK firms.

Question 17.4

Posco, the fourth largest steelmaker around the globe, and the Hyundai Heavy Industries Co., the biggest shipyard, bought shares in each other a few years ago.

Using the internet investigate the reasons for this decision.

Unit 18: **Government policy towards the private sector**

In recent years governments have wished to increase the role of the private sector in activities previously the sole preserve of the public sector, because they believe that this is conducive to the efficient use of economic resources. **Privatisation** is one example (see Unit 14); another is the **Private Finance Initiative (PFI)**, encouraging private investment in projects that once would have been state funded. **Public Private Partnerships (PPP)** is the umbrella name given to a range of initiatives which involve the private sector in the operation of public services, the PFI is the most widely used initiative.

The Private Finance Initiative (PFI)

Until relatively recently it was widely accepted that certain services, such as hospitals and prisons, should not only be delivered by the public sector, but also produced or provided by it. The PFI challenges this supposition, and successive governments believed that private sector finance and management expertise, combined with the profit incentive, enabled the private sector to produce services more cheaply than the public sector ever could.

In the majority of cases, the PFI involves the designing, financing, building and operation of capital assets such as hospitals and schools by the private sector. The private sector then secures a return on its investment in one of two ways. For some schemes, such as toll roads and bridges, the general public is charged as and when they use the facility. Examples include privately financed prisons where the public sector pays for the availability of prison cells. The north Birmingham relief road now called the 'M6 toll' is a high profile example of a PFI project in action where the user pays directly for the service provided to Midland Expressway Ltd who have a 50 year contract to operate the road. For others, the public sector is charged for the provision within the terms of the contact. Although the terms of PFI contracts vary a hospital built using the scheme would normally mean the NHS Trust paying an annual fee once the building is operational. This would be for possibly 30 years. Within the hospital cleaning, maintenance and catering would be provided by firms within the PFI consortium leaving the medical staff to carry out the clinical services. In theory a new hospital is provided without a large immediate burden on the taxpayer and the medical teams concentrate on their areas of expertise leaving ancillary services to the PFI consortium.

Figure 18.1: The cost of PFI

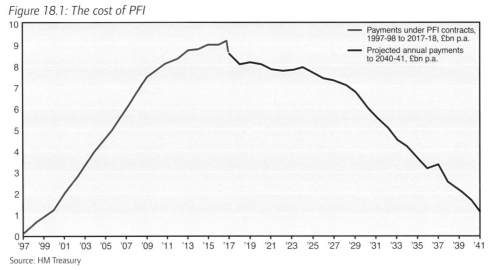

Source: HM Treasury

A limited number of PFI projects are funded by public private partnerships (PPP), although overall control of the project rests with the private sector. The public sector contribution is usually made to secure the wider social benefits (for example, road de-congestion) of a project that might not otherwise have gone ahead. The London Underground's investment programme was an example of PPP. Under the scheme, two engineering consortiums, Metronet and Tube Lines, won 30-year contracts worth £17bn to modernise the tracks, stations and tunnels, thereby splitting the tube's infrastructure from its operation, by London Underground. The private sector was to pay 25% towards the work, government grants 60% and fares 15%. However, the contract was so complex that it cost the taxpayer £455m in lawyers' and consultants' expenses just to draw it up! The deals were performance-related, so the companies were rewarded according to their success in reducing service delays. However since 2008 the underground network has been maintained by Transport for London (a public sector body), after Metronet went into administration. The whole 30 year project was plagued by delays and overspends as well as controversy over just how much better the tube network had become under Metronet's upgrade programme. Some blamed Metronet's shareholders for the collapse of the PPP arrangement but it had cost taxpayers £2bn.

Numerous doubts have been expressed about whether the theoretical benefits of the PFI can be delivered in practice. These include the possibility that high administration and costs, added to the fact that it is more expensive for the private sector to borrow than for the public sector, prevent PFI schemes making the planned cost savings. The public sector's borrowing costs are closely related to government bond yields while private sector firms borrow at higher market rates. Also, there are worries that private firms reduce the quality of buildings and services in order to reduce cost. There are, however, levels of service specified in contracts and the firms are penalised if these are not met. Perhaps the chief benefit of the scheme is that the risk of capital projects costing more than anticipated is no longer borne by the tax-payer. It is common for the cost of a project to escalate while it is in progress. If this happens during a PFI scheme, the private sector must meet the cost.

In recent years almost all new NHS hospitals and many state schools, prisons, roads and railways have been built with private-sector money. Most of the contracts last for about 25 years, with the Government paying for the buildings in stages. During the contract private firms are required to maintain the buildings to a high standard and keep them clean. Once the contract expires the building reverts to public sector ownership.

But Public Private Partnerships (PPPs), such as **contracting out** ancillary services to private firms, to taking over the management of a school, have been vigorously opposed by the trade unions. They say that public-sector staff who are transferred to the private sector have to work for less pay and in worse conditions. The PFI helps to reduce the level of government debt because borrowing by private companies under the scheme is not counted as government debt – off balance sheet. This poses a possible problem that the PFI is often preferred even when it is not the best option.

In October 2005 Britain's biggest Trade Union (Unison) demanded in its report 'A House Built on Sand' that the PFI be scrapped as the research that had been used to promote it was biased and manipulated. The then Labour government argued that although the PFI costs more in terms of building costs, it delivered value because it avoids overruns more than non-PFI work.

The poor state of the UK's public sector assets after years of under-investment had to be addressed. The alternative to PFI was higher government borrowing or increased taxation. This is an unpalatable alternative for those in government trying to improve the standard of the UK's public services.

In the recent recession many PFI schemes have encountered funding crises from construction companies and banks which form the consortiums which finance the projects. Work on schools, hospitals and road widening programmes have been delayed. Vince Cable, a long-time sceptic of PFI, said in 2009 that the government should go back to more traditional public financing structures rather than use taxpayers' money to prop up the public-private model. "We need to be very careful about the taxpayer taking all the risks and the private partners taking all the benefits."

When the coalition government was elected in 2010 there was a major re-think asking whether the PFI was in reality a very expensive way of providing much needed capital assets. Clearly some of the terms of PFI contracts were unfavourable with alarming examples of over-charging the public sector. Examples include a bill of £963 to install an aerial in the consultant's common room in a hospital. Further areas of apparent

poor value for money include the M25 road-widening project plus a number of Ministry of Defence contracts such as Air Tanker re-fuelling. Equally worrying for many is the selling of PFI equity in many of the 700 hospitals, schools and prisons that have been built under the scheme. If PFI is so lucrative to investors then the taxpayer is, according to some, losing out when it comes to value for money. In 2012 Peterborough City Hospital, built under a PFI scheme, was given a £46m bail-out little more than a year after it opened. The hospital is tens of millions of pounds in debt and has to pay the PFI consortium £3m per month as part of its contract. The 'FiReControl' project was designed to upgrade fire and rescue to nine regional control centres in England instead of 46 local control rooms. However the project was cancelled after problems with the IT system. The cost of this PFI project has reached £270m with rent, maintenance, water and electricity bills costing over £1m per month. Many of the buildings stand empty.

Contracting out

Communities around the world have in some cases improved quality and lowered cost by **contracting out** local services. Under this scheme, local authorities such as county and district councils act as enabling authorities that assess local needs and then specify the service they require. Bids are invited from in-house teams, voluntary organisations and private sector contractors. The emphasis shifts from the local council as a monopoly provider and manager, to the council as enabler and monitor of high standards. In theory the introduction of competition drives down costs, encourages innovation and improves standards. In the UK local authorities have contracted out to private firms such services as household rubbish collection, home support services and office catering. Although free marketers will support the idea of resources no longer being directed by 'the dead hand of the state' there is extensive evidence that lower costs are achieved by lower wages for staff accompanied by poorer terms of employment and inferior working conditions.

The process of awarding these contracts for local authority services was originally organised through **compulsory competitive tendering**. This was introduced in the 1980s, and local authorities were forced to open up in-house services, such as refuse collection and road maintenance, to private competition in order to effort to reduce costs and improve value for money. Compulsory competitive tendering was never popular because many believed that it placed too much emphasis on cutting costs at the expense of quality of service. Since 2000 compulsory competitive tendering has largely been replaced by what is called '**best value**'. Best value requires local authorities to deliver a continuous improvement in the standard and efficiency of their services, bringing in outside private firms where it is seen appropriate. **Competitive tendering** is still used by local authorities as evidenced by this quote from the Bracknell Forest Homes web site regarding the employment of an electrical contractor to complete the digital switchover for council houses in the area: "Bracknell Forest Homes has used a competitive tender process to select an experienced, qualified and best value contractor to do the installation work."

Government failure

Government failure occurs when government intervention, maybe to correct a market failure, has the effect of introducing a market distortion which causes allocative inefficiency. It is often assumed that once market failure has been identified it can be either reduced or eliminated through government intervention, for example, by imposing taxes, controls and regulation. This benign view of the role of the government in the economy centring on the use of public policy to correct market failure wherever it is found to exist illustrates what may be called the **public interest theory** of government behaviour. This theory argues that governments intervene in a benevolent fashion in the economy in order to eliminate waste and to achieve an efficient and socially desirable allocation of resources.

Public choice theory, however, looks at political decisions from the point of view of self-seeking or utility maximising politicians. If politicians are assumed to want to maximise their utility by maximising votes then they will not be very interested in the welfare of those who do not vote. If we assume that they wish to maximise the number of seats they win in the House of Commons, then they will be much more interested in the welfare of those in the marginal constituencies than those in the seats that never change hands. As soon as we admit that public choice theory is plausible, we have to admit that even a government with the correct information might reduce society's welfare when intervening in the market. For example, subsidies may prevent the exit of a firm from an industry, but preserve employment in a marginal parliamentary constituency.

Darker versions of public choice theory are possible and are sadly all too applicable to some countries. If we assume politicians have the objective of making money, then they will make decisions according to the highest bribe on offer. Governments take resources away from taxpayers and reallocate them. Any re-allocation of resources influenced by bribery is likely to be a very long way from welfare maximising from society's viewpoint.

Aside from direct state provision, the most well-known example of government intervention in the free market is the **Common Agricultural Policy (CAP)**. The main way that this works is by the setting of minimum prices for most agricultural products, including tobacco and wine. The original intention of the CAP was to counteract market failure.

Public choice theory provides a framework to explain the CAP. Those who ran the EU were serving the interests of food producers, not consumers. Farmers demonstrated frequently and sometimes violently near Brussels and often blocked roads. Consumers, who have lost so much from the CAP have never demonstrated against it. Those consumers who lose most from the CAP are the poor who spend the highest proportion of their income on food. The high prices to consumers and the consequent loss of consumer surplus coupled with tariffs to prevent cheap imports of food entering the EU impose allocative inefficiency on society. The market distortions of the CAP both within the EU and internationally in world agricultural markets are examples of collective government failure by the EU states, despite recent attempts at reform which have placed greater emphasis on income support rather than price support. Similarly the EU's Common Fisheries Policy, which set maximum quotas of certain species of fish which could be landed, produced allegations of government failure. Trawlers had to discard at sea dead or dying fish in order to remain within their quota. This policy too is being reformed.

Government failure may also occur through the over-taxing of demerit goods and negative externalities, and through the over-provision of public and merit goods. Heavy taxation of cigarettes has led to many people in the South-East of England taking a short ferry trip to France or Belgium to buy cheap cigarettes some of which are sold on to friends. High tax on petrol in Northern Ireland has led in the past to many people crossing the border into the Republic of Ireland to fill their tanks. This can be related to the 'law of unintended consequences' when a government policy (tax, regulation or subsidy) has an effect which is unanticipated. Would the government have banned smoking in public places if they had known how much it would have accelerated the decline of the pub trade with tens of pubs closing every week? Probably yes, but there would have been a few misgivings.

Many economists believe that some of the privatisations carried out in the 1980s and 1990s produced badly structured industries which have led to significant difficulties in recent years. This could arguably apply to the energy sector and the railways which are both large complex industries which may have been privatised more effectively using a different model. Regulation is made more difficult and government intervention has been significant in recent years as both sectors have faced major challenges. There is also an additional issue regarding ownership – should the UK government have allowed much of our water, energy and transport providers to fall into foreign ownership? Regulatory capture occurs when a regulatory body such as Ofwat and Ofgem appear to operate in favour of the vested interests of producers rather than consumers. It could be argued that regulators can often prevent the market operating freely. In many cases regulators may have insufficient information to adequately balance the interest of consumers, producers and investors and thus inevitably the result of regulation is flawed resulting in inefficient outcomes.

Government action does not have to lead to government failure. The most prosperous countries in the world generally have a large proportion of their GDP – anything from 30% to 50% – allocated by the public sector. Vast amounts of resources are allocated by governmental decision, often to deal with the perceived failure of the market to provide appropriate quantities of important goods and services. If governments sometimes make mistakes, that is not a good reason for pessimism and cynicism.

Question 18.1

In recent years many governments have felt that in order to reduce greenhouse gas emissions they should subsidise the production of biofuels so that they can reduce their dependence on fossil fuels. There was subsequently the accusation that this resulted in government failure. Examine the case for this assertion using the links below.

http://news.bbc.co.uk/1/hi/sci/tech/7758542.stm

http://news.bbc.co.uk/1/hi/uk/7581436.stm

Question 18.2

PFI or bust

by Ian Mulheirn

The Private Finance Initiative has been branded a rip-off, but it's still the only game in town. What we need is a more sensible approach to accounting for infrastructure investment.

Everyone seems to love to hate the Private Finance Initiative. This week, the Public Accounts Committee raised further **questions** about the cost effectiveness of the concept in a report claiming that the current model of **PFI doesn't offer value for money**. The charge sheet against PFI is getting longer: procurement processes aren't competitive, contracts are inflexible, whole-life costs don't appear to be lower, efforts to transfer risk may be flawed, and the completion of projects may even be slower than under conventional delivery. What's more, in the post-financial crisis world, it appears that the cost of capital for PFI projects may be twice that of government gilts. So it seems increasingly implausible to argue that PFI represents a good deal for taxpayers relative to conventional procurement.

Having established that a policy crime has been committed, recent select committee reports from both the Public Accounts and **Treasury** committees even go on to identify a motive. The Chancellor's second fiscal rule – that public sector net debt must be falling in 2015-16 – gives strong incentives for government to deploy PFI to keep infrastructure spending off the government's books. This was also an imperative of Gordon Brown's 40% of GDP sustainable investment rule. So it's deeply unfashionable to defend PFI at the moment. There are few legitimate benefits over conventional procurement, and, if wriggling out of fiscal rules can be described as a benefit, one nefarious one.

But branding PFI a rip-off isn't the same thing as concluding that we should stop doing it. There's little point in comparing PFI to some hypothetical alternative conventional funding approach. Rather we need to compare it to what would happen if PFI were disallowed. With the existing fiscal rules, if you can't build a school by PFI, it probably just won't get built at all, since departmental capital spending has been slashed. So the real comparison in most cases is between a pricey PFI hospital or no hospital at all. Whether it's worth the higher price-tag depends on the social value of the project compared to that cost.

Establishing the social value of such investment is all but impossible. But, as successive governments have been so keen on PFI – including ones that pilloried the concept in **Opposition** – it seems clear that society would prefer to have these things built than not, even if they do involve a large credit card bill. That successive governments feel the need to invent complicated private finance wheezes to get round their own fiscal rules only serves to underline the absurd incentives created by the way that investment spending is treated in the National Accounts.

The only real alternative that will achieve the desired level of investment is to unblock the public finance route by recognising publicly financed assets as such, rather than just counting their cost.

But unless and until that argument is resolved, it seems like PFI, or some variant of it, is the only game in town.

That argument would stand at any time but right now, with the economy in recession, it's more important than ever. The UK economy is trying to move from growth fuelled by government and household consumption, to growth powered by investment and exports. With the exports route closed off, the investment lever is the only one that government has to pull. Having boxed itself in on publicly financed investment, it needs to continue to find a way around its own rules in order to support output.

So PFI might be a rip-off, but less investment would be far worse than expensive investment at the moment. And until we have a more sensible approach to accounting for infrastructure investment, that looks like the choice we face. Perhaps the next select committee report should focus on tackling that underlying problem.

Source: Public Finance 4 May 2012   Social Market Foundation

Question: How could the government reform the PFI scheme?

Question 18.3

The case against PFI
The trade union UNISON believes there are a number of reasons for opposing PFI:

Reason 1: The public service ethos
Public services are not like other commodities. They exist to support the social, economic and environmental well being of communities and where a community decides that the market alone cannot provide a particular activity. The state then assumes some degree of responsibility for the service: by funding the service or by regulating for its quality and delivery. In a post election Mori poll for UNISON over 80% of people rejected the use of private companies to run public services.

Reason 2: PFI is driven by public finances not public services
PFI was conceived by a Conservative government that had lost control of public borrowing. The current government's desire to keep borrowing off the public sector balance sheet remains the main driver for PFI. Public authorities know that PFI is the only way to get finance, which partly explains the unspent millions in the public coffers. The Government can afford to pay for the entire PFI programme from its reserves.

Reason 3: PFI costs more
PFI schemes cost much more than conventionally funded projects. The private sector borrows at higher rates than the public sector since governments can borrow at much lower rates. Audit Scotland have calculated these costs as adding £0.2-£0.3 million each year for every £10 million invested. They have high set up costs, due to lengthy negotiations involving expensive city lawyers and consultants employed by both sides. The first 15 NHS trust hospitals spent £45 million on advisers an average of 4% of the capital value. The private sector demands high returns and despite very low risks, profits from PFI are extremely high.

There is a growing body of evidence that PFI projects escalate both in scale and cost. These are not simple cases of costs going up for a project but reflect the very nature of PFI itself. The higher costs inevitably lead to an affordability gap for the procuring authority that is often met by reductions in services and capacity, subsidies from other parts of public authority budgets and pressures on labour costs. A recent article in the British Medical Journal found that there were 20% cuts in staffing levels in PFI hospitals.

Reason 4: PFI profits from people

UNISON has conducted research into the impact of contracting out in local government on the terms and conditions of the workforce. UNISON's survey found evidence of a two-tier workforce, something commented on by both the Treasury and Health committees of the House of Commons.

- Over 90% of those contacted said pay levels for new employees were worse that for transferred staff.

- 1 in 5 of contracts showed a difference in the standard working week.

- Pensions are a high value item for employees and a high cost item for contractors and public authorities.

- Guidance from government means that successful contractors are obliged to offer a comparable pension scheme to transferred employees. Our research could not find a single comparable scheme open to new employees. There was either no scheme or else it was inferior and often the contractor made no contribution whatever.

- There is inevitably a gender impact with women increasingly bearing the brunt of these new privatisations, just as they did under CCT and market testing. PFI contracts are at least 25 years long. As the first tier gradually disappears and only those staff on private sector terms and conditions are left, there will be a whole class of women workers providing public services who will have no occupational pensions and who will be working on inferior terms and conditions.

Reason 5: PFI goes wrong

There have been many claims that the private sector is more efficient than the public sector but there is no evidence offered to support this. Now that PFI schemes are coming on stream there is growing evidence that they are not producing the anticipated improvements in delivery to time or cost nor are they meeting the quality standards expected. After all, many of the same companies that were involved in pre-PFI cost and time overruns are also building PFI schemes.

Reason 6: PFI does not give 'value for money'

For many PFI projects, it is only the transferred risks that make the project value for money. Research for UNISON by Professor Allyson Pollock, looking at schools and hospitals, shows that the calculations of risk are arbitrary and unreliable. The National Audit Office has called the value for money calculation "pseudo-scientific mumbo jumbo where the financial modeling takes over from thinking".

Reason 7: Private companies make unacceptable profits

As well as the huge returns made by private companies they are refinancing their deals and yielding huge profits at the expense of the public sector. The principal risks transferred to the private sector in PFI projects are those met during the construction phase, risks that disappear at an early stage of the project. Despite this, the risks are treated as if they were spread over the whole length of the contract and it is therefore very profitable for contractors to refinance projects. At Fazakerley prison the National Audit Office reported that the net result is that the rate of return for the initial shareholders has tripled from 12.8% at the start to 39%.

There has been extensive use of the Private Finance Initiative or Public Private Partnerships to allow private companies to raise money for major public service projects. But it costs more for private companies to raise money than it would for the government or local government. The only way private companies will make their money back is to cut either services or staffing costs. That means public service workers and users pay the real costs.

Source: Unison

Access the Unison web site and read other documents on this trade union's opposition to PFI. (www.unison.org.uk)